I Hear with my Little Ear

Liz Baldwin

Permission to photocopy

Acknowledgements

I have many people who have influenced my life as a speech-language therapist to thank: most notably my inspirational manager for many years, Michelle Morris, and my dear friends and colleagues Jean, Janet and Rachel.

I also thank my boys at home, Pete, Sam and Zac, who have been unstinting in their encouragement whilst I have been writing this book.

I Hear with my Little Ear
MT10143
ISBN-13: 978 1 85503 414 3
© Liz Baldwin
Illustrations © Theresa Tibbetts
All rights reserved
First published 2006
Reprinted 2007, 2008 (twice), 2009 (twice), 2010 (twice), 2011, 2013, 2014

Printed in the UK for LDA
Pintail Close, Victoria Business Park, Nottingham, NG4 2SG

MIX
Paper from
responsible sources
FSC
www.fsc.org   FSC® C023114

Contents

✪ Final sounds

✪ Rhyming

✪ Phoneme manipulation

✪ Photocopiable resources......128

Introduction to phonic skills

Listening to a spoken word and breaking it down into its component sounds is a fundamental skill for effective language learning. This skill develops long before children know anything about letters (graphemes) and sound being represented visually through graphemes. Young children are learning to analyse phonemes – individual units of sound that, when combined, make meaningful words. Poor phonological analysis skills may affect children in the following ways.

Development of literacy skills

Phonological analysis is widely recognised as the strongest predictor of literacy skills. Children may start reading and writing well, using the visual method of whole-word recognition. When they attempt to decode a new word, however, the visual method is not sufficient.

Development of language skills

To develop understanding of a word, children must listen to the word and lay down in their memory a representation of what it sounds like. Every time they hear that word they add meaning to it. When they lay down an incomplete or inaccurate representation of the word, the next time they hear it their memory store may not recognise it and the meaning is lost. These children are at risk of delay in the development of the understanding of spoken language, and likely to have a restricted spoken vocabulary.

Development of speech sounds

Difficulties with the phonological analysis of words may result in speech sound problems – phonological delay or disorder. The cause of many speech sound difficulties is not that children are unable to make the sounds physically but that their ability to analyse the sounds is restricted.

Phonological awareness is the ability to segment words into their components and build them up again. The child needs to segment to identify:

✪ single **words** spoken within a sentence;

✪ **syllables** within words;

✪ **initial sounds** (phonemes);

✪ **all other sounds** (phonemes) within the word.

They then need to be able to blend these sounds to say the word.

Using the games

The games in this book allow for opportunities to practise the phonological skills mentioned on page 6, and provide a balance between identification (of individual syllables and phonemes) and generation (of words according to target sounds).

Each game has suggestions for making the task harder or easier, helping you to pitch the game for your group or individual child's ability. It also enables you to revisit games later and make them stretch children's existing skills. They will not learn these skills through being constantly asked to do something they cannot do, so don't treat the games as a test. Intervene when they struggle: let them hear you working out sounds and let them experiment with making the sounds.

This resource is useful for consolidating existing phonological skills, stretching able children, and teaching those starting out on the phonological awareness journey. It is a rich source of activities for children who need to practise a particular skill before being able to use that skill independently.

The games are divided into sections. See the Contents page at the beginning for a complete list by sections. Children starting to learn about phonological awareness should begin with syllable work, move to word initial practice, then to word final sound and rhyme, and finally manipulation and deletion. This approach may not be necessary; you may use the book to enhance children's existing skills or target a particular area or group of sounds.

Usually, children will find identification of sounds easier than generation of words. It is vital that children are skilled in identification of sounds, and you are strongly recommended to choose some activities from each section to address this.

The games are designed to be played in group settings, enabling the children to learn in an interactive way and gain knowledge from their peers. It also makes the activities less threatening for the child who is struggling. They can be used with a whole class or a small group. They are equally appropriate for families at home. Speech and language therapists may use the games in group work or as part of a therapy package for school or home. They are designed to be led by teachers, teaching assistants, speech and language therapists and parents.

Above all, let the children have fun as they play with sounds.

Animal clap

Children learn how to count syllables by clapping them out.

⭐ Resources

None

⭐ How to play

This is a quick game to help fill a couple of minutes. Ask every child to think of an animal. Tell the children that they need to work out the number of syllables in that animal's name by clapping the corresponding number of times. Encourage them to listen to what others have said and not to repeat animal names that have already been used.

To make the game easier

Have some pictures of animals available, so the children can concentrate on counting syllables instead of generating vocabulary. After each child says their animal's name, the whole group claps it out together.

To make the game harder

Challenge the group to think of the animal name with the most number of syllables in it.

Variations

You can play this game with different categories, such as names of countries, fruits, vegetables, sports and television programmes.

Building blocks

This fun, interactive game is a great way for children to practise counting syllables.

⭐ Resources

Building blocks

⭐ How to play

This game is best suited to small groups. Put a pile of building blocks in the middle of the floor or table. Tell the group that they are going to practise counting syllables. You will say a word to each child in turn. Once you've said the word, that child must work out how many syllables are in the word and pick up the corresponding number of blocks. Continue playing with the next child. When all the blocks have been used up, the game is over and the children can build together with the blocks they have accumulated.

To make the game easier

When you say the word, encourage the group to say and clap it together. Once the group has worked out the number of syllables in the word, everyone takes the corresponding number of blocks.

To make the game harder

Rather than telling each child a word, show them a picture. This requires each child to apply their phonological knowledge.

Jumping jack

In this active game the children will learn how to practise breaking words into syllables.

⭐ Resources

Four big hoops; if you don't have any hoops, you can make large circles from pieces of string.

⭐ How to play

Arrange the hoops in a line. Tell the group that they're going to play a syllable game. To play the game they must jump through one hoop for each syllable in their name. For instance, Thomas will jump through two hoops, Jamallah will jump through three hoops, and so on.

Before asking the children to jump through the hoops, it may be helpful to demonstrate this activity with your name. Once the group is ready to jump through the hoops, ask them each to say their name and to try to divide it into syllables. Then ask them to jump through the hoops in turn and say their name at the same time.

When a child has finished jumping through the hoops and has said their name, count and say the number of hoops they have jumped through. Then ask them to confirm how many syllables there are in their name.

You may decide that everyone in the group should say the child's name as they jump. This will hold everyone's attention and help the children hear the syllables.

Depending on the size of your group and the time available, you could choose a few children to take part each day, until the entire group has joined in.

To make the game easier

Before a child jumps through the hoops, demonstrate how to break their name into syllables: Ab-dul, Mel-lis-sa, Ham-al, and so on. After this, ask the child to say their name independently and jump through the hoops. Alternatively, the child could ask a friend to help them divide their name into syllables.

To make the game harder

Ask the child to jump and say, for instance, 'My name is Sam' or 'My name is Sam Brown' or even 'My name is Sam Martin Brown.' You will need more than four hoops to play the game.

Food numbers

This game improves the children's ability to count syllables.

⭐ Resources

Three boxes: one marked 1, another marked 2 and the last marked 3; coloured pencils and paper

⭐ How to play

Distribute a pencil and a piece of paper to each child. Ask each group to draw a fruit or vegetable. Encourage the group to try to think of a fruit or vegetable that no one else will choose. After the children have finished drawing their picture, choose a couple of volunteers to stand up and say the name of their fruit or vegetable. They must also say how many syllables are in the word. Next, the child puts the drawing into Box 1, 2 or 3, depending on the number of syllables in the word. You could encourage the rest of the group to say and clap each word together at this point to keep their attention.

To make the game easier

Rather than have the children work independently, pair them up with another child.

To make the game harder

To make this a more challenging task that relies on internal phonic knowledge, ask the children to work out the number of syllables in the word without saying it. Then have the children put their pictures in the corresponding box as explained above.

Clap it

This is a great game to develop team work and teach the children how to count syllables.

⭐ Resources

Picture cards showing items whose names have a different number of syllables (page 128).

⭐ How to play

Split the children into two groups. Use twelve picture cards. Display three of them, one with one syllable, one with two syllables and one with three syllables. Choose one group to start. That group decides amongst themselves which picture they want to divide syllabically. One person is chosen from the team to clap the number of syllables in that picture. For instance, a child would clap twice for the word **table** and once for the word **cat**. The opposing team must work out what picture has been clapped. If the opposing team can identify the correct picture, it is removed and replaced with another picture with the same number of syllables. The teams take turns to clap for each other. Continue until all the pictures have been used.

Award points to a team for clapping the correct number of syllables and working well together.

To make the game easier

Display pictures with only one or two syllables for the teams.

To make the game harder

Award extra points to a team if the child who is clapping includes a stress on the stressed syllable: com *put* er, *ta* ble, *li* brar y, and so on.

Spin to win

Children will enjoy racing their peers to discover the number of syllables in a word.

⭐ Resources

A large, round piece of paper divided into three parts and labelled 1, 2, 3; bottle to act as a spinner; one picture with one, two or three syllables for each child (page 128)

⭐ How to play

Ask the children to sit in a circle. Give each child a picture and tell them to put the picture in front of them where the rest of the group can see it. Place the piece of paper and the bottle in the middle of the circle, and choose one person to spin the bottle. Each child's task is to determine if the bottle lands on a number that matches the number of syllables in their picture. If it does, they have to be the first one to put their hand up to be the winner of that round. If their picture does match the number of syllables on the spinner, it is turned face down. The child who wins the round spins the bottle next. The game continues until all the children's pictures have been used.

To make the game easier

Have the children go round the circle before the game starts, and say and clap the number of syllables in their picture.

To make the game harder

Use pictures that have more than three syllables. You will need to adjust the numbers on your spinner accordingly. Items to use include these:

✪ alligator	✪ hippopotamus	✪ supermarket
✪ asparagus	✪ photographer	✪ television
✪ avocado	✪ refrigerator	✪ thermometer
✪ caterpillar	✪ rhinoceros	✪ watermelon

Syllable bingo

This listening game will improve the children's awareness of syllables in words.

⭐ Resources

Blank bingo cards (page 129); counters

⭐ How to play

Give each child a blank bingo card and a set of ten counters. Ask them to write 1, 2 and 3 in various squares on the bingo card until the card is filled. Explain that the numbers on the grid are for the number of syllables in a word. When you say a word, the children must work out the number of syllables in that word and cover the corresponding number on their card with a counter. When they have four counters in a diagonal, horizontal or vertical row, they shout 'Bingo!' The first to do that is the winner of the game.

Use this game as an opportunity to say words that don't have a picture stimulus. For instance, use adjectives, prepositions and verbs as part of the game. Consider using target words that are about to be introduced in spelling or reading assignments.

To make the game easier

Instead of giving each child their own bingo card, have them work in pairs or small groups, so that they can help each other.

Encourage the children to repeat the word after you've said it. In addition, you could ask the group to clap the word out, in order to understand better how to break it into syllables.

To make the game harder

Ask the children to work out the number of syllables in the word without saying it, thus testing their ability to segment words in their heads.

Syllable lotto

The children will enjoy matching number cards to pictures by the number of syllables.

⭐ Resources

Pictures with one, two or three syllables (see page 128); number cards marked 1, 2 or 3; sticky tape

⭐ How to play

Make a number card with a matching number of syllables for each picture you've chosen for this game. For example, **ball** needs to have a no. 1 card, **ruler** needs to have a no. 2 card. Stick all the pictures up on a wall. Ask the children to name the pictures and clap the syllables in each word. Spread the number cards face down in front of the group. Choose one child to turn over a card. Tell them to look at the number on the card and to find a picture with the corresponding number of syllables. For instance, for the number 3 they might choose a picture of an elephant, banana or computer. Tape the number card under the picture. Ask the next child to turn over a number card. Continue playing the game until all the pictures have a number card underneath them.

To make the game easier

Reduce the number of choices by having only one picture with one syllable, one picture with two syllables and one picture with three syllables on display at any one time. With a reduced number of choices, the group will have a better chance of success.

If necessary, start the game using only one- and two-syllable words, and gradually work up to three syllables.

To make the game harder

Choose words with more syllables to add to the level of difficulty. For this, it will be necessary to make different number cards.

Syllable rhythms

This fun game uses musical instruments and rhythm to help children count syllables.

⭐ Resources

Musical instruments; picture cards of items with a different number of syllables (see page 128). You could also use pictures from magazines, the Internet or clip art software.

⭐ How to play

Give each child a musical instrument such as a drum, xylophone, maracas or guitar. Ask the group to practise making one, two and three sounds on their instrument. Explain that words, like music, have a rhythm to them and can be broken into syllables. Say a word with more than one syllable, and ask the group to repeat the word and to shake, pluck or hit their instrument at the same time. Next, show the children a picture of that word and ask them to say the word and make a sound with their instrument according to the number of syllables it has. The activity is over when all the pictures have been used.

Depending on the size of your group, you may want to do this activity in small groups each day until every child has had a chance to participate.

To make the game easier

Before starting the activity, show the group all of the picture cards. Name all of the picture cards with the group, so that they can hear you breaking the words into syllables. After the children have had practice doing this with you, try playing the game as explained above.

To make the game harder

Ask the children to work out the number of syllables in a word without saying it. Challenge them to see if they can work out which is the stressed syllable in each word – for instance, *cat* er pil lar, com *put* er.

Mystery rule

Children will enjoy trying to work out your mystery rule while learning how to count syllables.

⭐ Resources

None

⭐ How to play

In this game you will create a mystery rule that is to do with syllables. One example of a mystery rule is that only children with two syllables in their name may sit down. Ask the group to stand up. Tell the children that you have invented a mystery rule for the class and that it has something to do with their names. Only those that abide by the rule can sit down. Each child will ask you if they may sit down. You will tell them 'yes' or 'no', according to your rule. Continue playing the game until one of the children has worked out what your rule is.

To make the game easier

Before playing the game, tell the class that the rule has something to do with syllables. It may be helpful for the children to clap the number of syllables in their name before beginning the game. This will give them a better idea of how words can be divided and broken apart into syllables.

To make the game harder

Include surnames in your rule. Ask the children to do all their working out in their heads and not to say their name or clap it out.

Out of the hat

This game helps children learn how to count syllables.

⭐ Resources

Everyday items that will fit in a hat, such as a pen, ruler, paperclip, brick, glove, pencil sharpener, necklace and calculator; hat

⭐ How to play

Put all of the items in the hat. Ask the children to take a turn to pull an item out of the hat. Once the item has been removed, the child should name the item and clap the number of syllables in the word. Continue playing until all the items have been pulled out of the hat.

To make the game easier

After a child has pulled an item out of the hat, ask the whole group to say the word and clap the number of syllables in it.

To make the game harder

After a child pulls an item out of the hat, ask them to tell you how many syllables there are in the word without saying it. The rest of the group must then decide whether the answer was correct by saying and clapping the word.

Robot talk

Children will enjoy speaking in a robot voice while learning how to break words into syllables.

⭐ Resources

None

⭐ How to play

Robot talk is characterised by speaking one syllable at a time in a monotone. Introduce yourself in a robot voice: 'My-name-is-Miss-us-John-son.' Ask the children, one by one, to introduce themselves in a robot voice.

Once the group understands how to talk like a robot, begin asking them questions and request that they answer you in a robot voice. It is best if you continue modelling robot talk when you ask them the questions. For instance, 'What-did-you-do-on-your-hol-i-day?'

To make the game easier

Ask the children short questions and integrate some movement with each syllable, such as marching, clapping or finger counting.

To make the game harder

Pair the children and ask them to have a conversation in robot talk. The first child to slip out of robot talk is the loser.

Roll it

Using a die and picture cues, children will learn how to determine the number of syllables in a word.

⭐ Resources

A die with the numbers 1, 2, 3, 1, 2, 3 (page 130). You will need to mark the numbers on the die.

⭐ How to play

Arrange the children in a circle and ask them to sit down. Give one child a die and ask them to roll it. The child's task is to think of a word with the number of syllables corresponding to the number shown on the die. For instance, if they roll a 2 they could say **table**, **apple** or **balloon**. You could suggest that the group look around the room to find their words.

Encourage the children to say the word and clap out the syllables in it.

To make the game easier

Gather a selection of items with one, two or three syllables. Put the items in the middle of the circle and ask the child to select an item with the correct number of syllables for the number they have rolled. Once an item has been selected, remove it from the circle and replace it with another item with the same number of syllables.

To make the game harder

Use a die with the numbers 1 to 6 on it. Ask the children to come up with an adjective–noun description of the correct syllable length. For instance, the child could say 'yellow ruler' if they rolled a 4, 'colourful classroom' if they rolled a 5, and so on. Keep in mind that this activity may require modelling from you before the children attempt to make their own descriptions.

Number lines

In this game, the children use number lines to help them generate phrases of varying syllable length.

⭐ Resources

A number line for each child (see page 131)

⭐ How to play

Give each child a number line. Chose a number from 1 to 10 and ask the children to make up a phrase (or sentence) with that number of syllables. Encourage the group to use the number line to assist them when counting the syllables. It may be necessary to demonstrate how to play this game by modelling the game on your own number line. For instance, if you choose the number 6 you could say something like 'I am very happy', 'My mum has gone shopping', or 'The dog is black and white.'

Ask a few children to pair up and share their phrase with the rest of the group. To engage everyone, you may want to encourage the whole group to join in by clapping each syllable in the phrase. Continue playing the game by choosing a different number.

To make the game easier

Give the children a starter such as:

✪ I am …
✪ My cat …
✪ Today is …
✪ Are you …?

To make the game harder

Challenge each child to work at a higher level of phonological skill by not saying their phrase out loud until they are asked to share it with the group.

Paper planes

This is a fun game, in which the children are thinking about syllables in words.

⭐ Resources

Pencils and paper

⭐ How to play

Give each child a pencil and paper. Instruct them to make a paper aeroplane. Say a number between 1 and 3 and tell the children to draw a picture corresponding to a word with that number of syllables in it. For example, if you said 'two' the children might draw a picture of a donkey, carrot or finger.

When the group have finished their drawings, they launch their planes on the count of 3. Each child then picks up an aeroplane made by someone else and has a look at the picture. Go round the group and ask the children to name the picture they have picked up. How many syllables does it have? Encourage them to clap or stamp the number of syllables in the word. Choose a different number and ask the children to draw another picture on their new paper aeroplane. Repeat the game until the children are familiar with counting syllables in words.

To make the game easier

Before beginning, brainstorm a list of words with one or two syllables. Record the words on a flipchart and then play the game as explained above, but restrict the choice of words by using only those with one or two syllables. The children who find it difficult to generate a word can refer to the flipchart; others can generate their own words.

To make the game harder

In addition, ask the children to draw pictures for words with specific initial sounds or final sounds, or that rhyme with a word you supply.

Snakes and ladders

Using the familiar game Snakes and Ladders, students will improve their ability to count syllables in words.

⭐ Resources

A Snakes and Ladders game board; four counters; pictures with varying numbers of syllables (see page 128). We have provided some pictures to help you get started. However, you may choose to extend the game with pictures from magazines, the Internet or clip art software.

⭐ How to play

This game is best suited to groups of four or fewer. The children play Snakes and Ladders in the usual way, but instead of a die they use a pile of pictures stacked face down. Each child takes a turn to turn over a picture and work out the number of syllables in it. They then move the corresponding number of spaces on the game board. For instance, if a child turns over a picture of a pineapple, they move their counter three spaces. Encourage the group to clap out the word while saying it to help them.

To make the game easier

Each child takes a turn to turn over a picture, but when the picture is turned over, all the children say the word and clap the number of syllables together. You could further simplify the game by using pictures of words with only one or two syllables.

To make the game harder

Challenge the children to work out the number of syllables in their head, without saying or clapping the word, thus requiring them to work at a higher phonological level. Alternatively, you could ask the group to say and clap a description for each picture, such as 'red table' or 'little mouse'. Remind them that the longer their phrase is, the more likely they are to win the game.

Ten steps

Children will enjoy this active game which teaches them how to count syllables.

⭐ Resources

Chalk; open play area

⭐ How to play

Split the children into four teams and ask them to form four lines. Depending on the size of your group and the time available, you may make the teams larger or smaller. Give each team a piece of chalk and appoint one person from each to draw a ladder with ten steps on a suitable surface. They can also be the score keeper. If you play inside, you can mark an area with tape, or use ten hoops for steps. Tell the group that the aim is to call words in turn to the first child in the line, who is the climber. The climber must move one step for each syllable. When a child has climbed all ten steps they win a point for the team. That child then moves to the back of the line and the next child becomes the climber. The game continues until all children have been a climber.

You can give each team a category to think of, such as children's names, sports, television programmes or pop idols. It may be necessary to give a new category each time a new player begins climbing the ladder.

To make the game easier

Give each team a selection of pictures to call to the climber, who then has to decide how many syllables there are in the word.

To make the game harder

Encourage the children who are calling the words to say a short description such as 'little carrot' or 'furry dog'. Remind the team that they will earn points more quickly if they choose long descriptions.

Running to sound

This energetic game is a great way to reinforce initial word sounds.

⭐ Resources

Letter cards; sticky tape

⭐ How to play

Put a letter card into each of the four corners of the hall. Arrange the group into four teams, adjusting this depending on the size of your group. Tell the children that when it is their team's turn, you will say a word starting with one of the four letters displayed. The group must work out what letter the word starts with and run to the corresponding corner of the hall. You can make variations by asking the team to hop, jump, skip or walk when it is their turn.

To make the game easier

Reduce the number of choices the teams make by putting only two sounds in the hall. Start the game by saying sounds in isolation, such as **mmmm** rather than **moon**. Once the children are able to respond to single sounds, try saying simple consonant–vowel combinations such as **my, mo, me**, and so on. Keep in mind that for the purposes of this game nonsense words are acceptable.

To make the game harder

Choose multisyllabic words to add to the level of difficulty of the game. You can ask some of the children from the group to generate words for the rest.

Bingo

This game for a large group helps children detect the initial sounds in words.

⭐ Resources

Letter cards

⭐ How to play

Give each one of sixteen children a different letter card. Arrange the children so that they are sitting in a 4 by 4 square, with the rest alongside. Tell the children that you are going to say a word. If the first sound of that word matches the sound on their card, the children in the square must turn the card over. The game continues in the same way until one of the children on the sidelines notices that there are four cards in a line vertically, horizontally or diagonally and shouts 'Bingo!'

Repeat the game, ensuring that all children get an opportunity to sit in the square and are given different sound cards with which to play. Take advantage of the fact that no pictures are needed for this game by using words that are not nouns, such as **come**, **do**, **sigh**, **yes**, **think** and **behave**.

To make the game easier

Say the word, and ask the whole group to decide what the first sound is. Once the group has determined the initial sound, match the sound to the child who has the corresponding letter card. You may want to ask 'Who has **d** on their card?'

To make the game harder

Choose words with more syllables to increase the level of difficulty. An additional challenge is to ask the children sitting on the sidelines to say the words that begin with the initial sounds. That child must then determine if the correct card has been turned over in the bingo grid.

Book worms

Children will enjoy using pictures to help them identify initial sounds in words.

⭐ Resources

Picture books and a puppet; pens and paper

⭐ How to play

Choose a large book with plenty of pictures. Introduce your puppet, who loves looking for pictures that start with a target sound, such as **t**. Ask the children to help the puppet find all the pictures in the book that start with **t**, such as table, till, toffee and T-shirt. The children can keep a tally on scrap paper of how many pictures they find with the target sound. On another day, ask the children to help the puppet find pictures beginning with a different target sound.

To make the game easier

You can refine the search to a small part of the page and provide some clues, such as 'I see something beginning with **t** and it's something you can play with.'

To make the game harder

The puppet can try to confuse the children by suggesting words that don't start with the target sound. Do the children notice? Can they tell the puppet what sound the picture *does* start with?

Catch and say

This active game helps children generate words with an initial target sound.

⭐ Resources

Ball or beanbag

⭐ How to play

Ask the children to stand in a circle. Tell them that this game requires them to think of a word that starts with a target sound, such as **p**. Throw the ball or beanbag to one of the children and ask them to say a word beginning with **p**. After the child has said their word, they throw the ball to another person in the group, and the game continues as explained above. If someone is unable to think of a word, they can still throw the ball to another child, but they must sit down. The game continues until there is only one child left standing.

Depending on how much time is available, the last child standing could choose the next sound with which to play the game. The game would then start again with all of the children rejoining the circle.

To make the game easier

If a child cannot think of a word, you can give them clues such as 'I can think of a sharp thing that joins other things together' (pin). You may also want to hang up some pictures beginning with the target sound to help the group generate words.

To make the game harder

Ask each child to say their word before you count to 3, as working with a time limit makes the task more challenging.

Drawing sounds

Children will enjoy using their artistic skills while practising initial sounds in this game.

⭐ Resources

Pencils and paper; pictures that include many items that start with the same sound (see page 132). You could also use pictures from magazines, the Internet or clip art software.

⭐ How to play

Show the children a picture that includes many items that start with the same sound. Ask them to work out what sound that is, and to find all the items beginning with it. Next, ask the children to draw their own picture, including as many things as they can that begin with that sound. Ask them to show their pictures to one another. The pictures can be displayed to reinforce their knowledge of initial sounds. This activity works particularly well if the pictures are based around a theme, for instance, a kitchen.

To make the game easier

Brainstorm with the children a group of words that can be drawn on a large sheet of paper. After this, the children draw their own pictures with the list of words provided.

Alternatively, you can begin drafting on a large sheet of paper a picture with things that begin with the target sound. As the children become confident with their knowledge of that sound, they can come forward to draw in the same way. This gets them listening to one another. In addition, it helps them judge whether the drawings begin with the target sound.

To make the game harder

Give the children two target sounds. Ask them to draw words beginning with each sound on their own sheet of paper. Encourage the group to do this silently so that they are relying on their own phonic knowledge.

Finger count

This simple game is a great way to determine if your children need additional practice with initial letter sounds.

⭐ Resources

None

⭐ How to play

Begin the game by choosing a letter sound which you have previously introduced to the group. Tell the children that they must think of five words beginning with that sound as quickly as possible. The first child to raise their hand, with a word for each finger, is the winner.

To make the game easier

Ask the children to work in pairs to find their five words. If this game follows the introduction of a new sound, display any pictures you have used for the introduction, so that the children can use them as clues.

To make the game harder

Challenge the group to see if they can generate the five words within a minute or so. Additionally, you may consider asking the children to work in silence, which forces them to make this activity more of a mental task.

Feeling for sound

This exciting game makes use of tactile objects to help children find words beginning with the same sound.

⭐ Resources

A cloth bag into which the group cannot see; a number of objects to go in the bag that all begin with the same sound, and the same number of objects that begin with various other sounds

⭐ How to play

Show the group your bag and explain to them that there are a number of objects inside it. Tell them that you need their help with sorting out which things in the bag start with the target sound, such as **b**, and which things don't start with **b**. As each child puts their hand into the bag, encourage them to name what they think they can feel and to decide which sound that object starts with. The child must then remove the item and put it in the pile into which they think it belongs. Depending on the size of the group, the rest of the children could help identify the item, based upon their knowledge of the target sound as well as the child's description of it.

When the bag is empty, you should have a pile of things beginning with **b** and a pile of things that don't. As a group, name the things in the **b** pile and check whether or not they belong there. When all the items have been sorted, ask the children to generate more words that begin with the target sound.

Select individual children to participate in this activity each day until everyone in the group has had a chance to do so.

To make the game easier

Ask each child to remove an object from the bag. With your help, the child works out the initial sound of the chosen item. It may be necessary to exaggerate the first sound in the word. If the child is still struggling to identify the first sound of the object correctly, provide a forced alternative such as 'Does it start with **b** or **s**?'

When selecting the items that go in the bag, it is advisable to select things that start with contrasting sounds. For instance, **b** has a short sound, so you should contrast this with objects that start with long sounds such as **s**, **f**, **sh**, **m** or **l**.

To make the game harder

As the child reaches into the bag to select an object, ask them to work out the initial sound of the item without saying the word out loud. This strategy forces the child to rely on their knowledge of word structure, thus making it a more difficult task.

I hear with my little ear

In this game the children identify words by initial sounds.

⭐ Resources

None

⭐ How to play

Tell the children that you are going to play a listening game, and their job is to find something in the room that begins with the sound you say. Begin by saying 'I hear with my little ear, something beginning with …' and choose a sound such as **p**, **sh** or **f**. If a child correctly identifies an object that starts with the target sound, repeat the game with a different sound. If the child chooses an object that begins with the wrong sound, work out together what sound the object does begin with, remind them of your sound, and move on.

To make the game easier

Play the game as explained above, but put out a number of objects in front of the group. Take care when choosing the items because items beginning with **p** and **b**, for example, will be more difficult to discriminate between than objects beginning with **sh** and **g**. Before beginning, name all of the objects and if necessary work out the initial sounds of each together. If children struggle with this, give them a choice of two words and say something like 'I hear with my little ear, something beginning with **m**. Is it mat or cup?'

To make the game harder

Play the game as explained above. In this instance, encourage the children to list things with the target sound that may not be in the room. You can further challenge them by asking them to limit their choice of words to a category such as animals, fruit or people's names.

I went to the supermarket

This game is an excellent way to practise initial word sounds while improving your group's vocabulary and memory skills.

⭐ Resources

None

⭐ How to play

Tell the children that they are going to create a shopping list of things they can buy at the supermarket. The restriction, however, is that all of the things they add to the shopping list must begin with a target sound, such as **p**. You can begin the game by saying 'I went to the supermarket and bought some pencils.' The next child then repeats your sentence, but adds another item to the shopping list. For instance, they might say 'I went to the supermarket and bought some pencils and a peach.' The game continues until there are ten items on the shopping list.

Depending on the size of your group, you might want to create a shopping list with more than ten items. Alternatively, you could start the game again but use a different target sound for the next ten children in your group.

To make the game easier

Have a selection of items you might find in a supermarket available. This will make it easier for the children to choose words. Provide clues for items that could be added to the list. For example, for the word **potato** you could say 'I'm thinking of something beginning with **p**. It is a vegetable you can mash or make into chips.'

To make the game harder

Reduce the number of categories available to choose from. For instance, the shopping list might only include food items.

Let me show you

Children will enjoy working with their peers as they generate words with the same initial sound.

✪ Resources

Pictures for miming. You could use pictures from magazines, the Internet or clip art software.

✪ How to play

Divide the children into groups of about six, depending on the size of your group. Ask them to sit in a circle in their groups. Place a pile of pictures face down in the middle of each circle, one for each child. Select one child from each group to turn over a picture without showing it to the rest. That child should then tell their team the first sound of their picture and mime it for them. When a team has correctly identified the picture, they win a point. Continue playing until each child has mimed their picture.

To make the game easier

Choose pictures that relate to a certain theme, such as farm animals, sports or different jobs. Before starting the game, discuss the themes.

To make the game harder

Tell the teams that they will be awarded extra points for working out the other sounds in the word. For instance, if the picture is of someone who is smiling, they will get extra points if they identify **m** or **l** in the word.

Possible picture list

✪ jump	✪ smile	✪ cat	✪ dentist
✪ run	✪ cry	✪ elephant	✪ builder
✪ kick	✪ walk	✪ snake	✪ hairdresser
✪ hit	✪ hug	✪ rabbit	✪ footballer
✪ throw	✪ swim	✪ fish	

Register time

In this game, children will explore the first letter in their name and discover who else in the group shares it.

⭐ Resources

Letter cards

⭐ How to play

Spread out the letters of the alphabet on the floor of the room. Ask the children to stand next to the first letter of their name. Let them take a minute or so to discover who else has a name starting with the same letter as theirs. Ask them to find out if the letter they are standing next to matches the sound that their name starts with. For instance, Sarah and Seamus start with the same letter but have a different initial sound, as do Theo and Talia.

Next, ask the children to stand next to the letter that their surname begins with and explore the same possibilities as above. The game can continue with different criteria each time. For instance, the group could stand next to the first letter of their brother or sister's name, street address, pet's name or favourite snack.

To make the game easier

Encourage the children to work out the first letter or sound in their name before starting the game. In addition to putting out letters of the alphabet on the floor, add phonemes such as **sh** and **th** and discuss these with the group.

To make the game harder

Ask the group to generate names for the letters that have no one standing next to them. For instance, if there is no one whose name starts with **r**, the children might say Rose, Rashid, Rebecca and Ravi.

Word work

In this game the children will enjoy working in teams to generate words beginning with the same sounds.

⭐ Resources

One die with phonemes written on it (see page 130), one die with numbers 1 to 6 on it

⭐ How to play

Put the children into teams of six. Choose one member of the team to roll the two dice. The letter die determines what letter the words should begin with and the number die determines how many words with that initial sound the team must generate. If the first child rolls the letter **f** and the number 3, their team has to think of three words beginning with **f**, such as **fish**, **finger** and **four**. The team is awarded a point for each word. Choose one person from each team to be the score keeper. After the group has finished, they pass the dice to the next group. The first team to reach twenty points wins.

Depending on the size of your group and the time available, you may decide to make the teams larger or smaller and to give each team their own set of dice.

To make the game easier

Give the children clues for words if they are struggling to generate their own. For instance, if the target sound is **f**, you might say 'I can think of something that swims in water and begins with **f**.'

To make the game harder

Use a timer, and tell each group that they have only one minute to think of their words.

Alliteration time

Children will learn about alliteration in this game by making silly sentences.

⭐ Resources

Pens and paper; flipchart

⭐ How to play

Say some alliterative sentences for the group to hear. Here are some examples:

- ✪ Pete pats poodles.
- ✪ Tariq tickles turtle's toes.
- ✪ Four fat fish feast furiously on food.
- ✪ Sarah swims across the sea with seven seals.

Ask the children what sounds they hear repeated in each sentence. Write each sentence down on a flipchart and ask some volunteers to underline the target sound in a sentence. Put the children in pairs or in small groups and ask them to write their own sentence with the same sound repeated.

After each group has finished their task, let them share their sentences with the remainder of the group. Discuss who has made the longest alliterative sentence or whose sentence was the funniest.

To make the game easier

Introduce the idea of alliteration at a two-word level, such as: six socks, pink parcels, tall towers. Give each group the first word of a pair to help them generate the next word: mucky …, round …, five … .

To make the game harder

Ask the children to create a sentence with a minimum number of words that begin with the target sound. Challenge the children by asking them to make their sentences tell a story.

Sandy sounds

Children will enjoy using tactile objects to form letters and words in this activity.

⭐ Resources

Sand, beans or seeds; a tray

⭐ How to play

This game is best suited to individuals or small groups. Spread the sand out evenly onto a tray and ask a child to write a letter in the sand. Then ask the child to think of a word beginning with that sound. Can the rest of the group think of other words beginning with that sound?

Ask another child to come to the tray, rub the first letter out and write a different letter. Then ask them to think of a word beginning with that sound. You can vary this activity by using seeds or beans and asking the child to arrange the seeds or beans into the letter shape. This combination of fine motor movements and phonic sounds is a useful way to link letters and sounds.

To make the game easier

Start the activity by asking the child to write the first letter of their name. Encourage the group to think of other words that begin with the same sound.

To make the game harder

In addition to asking the children to think of a word that begins with the letter they've written, ask them to think of a word that ends with that letter.

Shopping game

The children work out initial sounds of various food items while shopping.

⭐ Resources

Pictures of food items (see page 133); carrier bags or baskets

⭐ How to play

Display the food pictures so that they are easily visible. Choose one child with a good grasp of letter sounds to be the check-out person. Put the rest in pairs and give them a carrier bag. Tell each pair to go shopping for food items that begin with a different sound. The checker decides whether all the food items in the carrier bags begin with the correct sound.

To make the game easier

Reduce the number of choices the children select from by asking them to find just one item beginning with the target sound. You could prompt them by saying something like 'Banana and cake. Which one starts with **b**?'

To make the game harder

The children work on their own. Tell them to work out silently what foods begin with the target sound. This makes them rely on their knowledge of phonetic properties.

Suggested picture list

- ✪ b: banana, bread, butter, biscuit, broccoli
- ✪ s: syrup, strawberries, squash, spaghetti
- ✪ c: carrots, cauliflower, cake, coffee, coke, cocoa, crisps
- ✪ m: milk, marshmallows, marmalade, muffin, meat, meatballs
- ✪ p: pizza, peach, pumpkin, peas, pear, popcorn, potato, pineapple
- ✪ ch: cheese, chips, chocolate, chicken, cherries
- ✪ l: lettuce, lemon, lime, lollipop, lamb chops

Sound stories

This game will not only improve the children's listening skills but will also help them identify initial sounds in the context of sentences.

⭐ Resources

Story book

⭐ How to play

Tell the children that you are going to read them a story. Every time they hear a word beginning with a target sound such as **h**, they should raise their hand. Appoint one child to keep a tally of the number of words with the target sound. Keep in mind that you will probably need to pause or exaggerate the pronunciation of the target words to help the children hear them.

To make the game easier

Read the story one sentence at a time. After each sentence, pause to discuss with the group whether or not they heard any words beginning with the target sound. You could start this game by using pictures and describing them.

To make the game harder

Divide the children into two groups. Give each group a different target sound to listen for. Tell the two groups that they will compete to see which team can hear more of the target sounds in the story. Points are awarded for correctly identifying words with the target sound, whereas points are deducted if a team puts their hands up for a word that does not start with the target sound. Alternatively you can let the children work individually, and keep their tally of words on a whiteboard with a dry erase marker.

Think and draw

This game encourages the children to generate words beginning with a target sound.

⭐ Resources

Large pieces of paper and pencils

⭐ How to play

Divide the group into teams of four to six children each. Depending on the size of your group, you may need to make the teams smaller or larger. Give each child a pencil and give each group one large sheet of paper to share. When you say a sound, each of the children in the group must quickly think of something to draw that begins with that sound. Allow them a minute to draw what they have thought of. The team gets a point if they draw a word beginning with the target sound that no one from any of the other teams draws. This is important because it encourages the children to think of words that are out of the ordinary. Keep the pace of the game quick so that the interest of the children is maintained. Continue the game for up to six turns, adding up the scores as you go along.

To make the game easier

Allow any picture that starts with the correct sound to be given a point.

To make the game harder

Don't allow the children to discuss with their team members whether or not their word begins with the target sound. This encourages the children to rely on their own phonic knowledge.

Word mime

This fun adaptation of charades is a great way to teach children about initial sounds in words.

★ Resources

Pictures. You could use pictures from magazines, the Internet or clip art software.

★ How to play

Tell the children that you are going to mime a picture and they must guess what it is. Start by giving the group a phonic clue such as 'It begins with **d**' and then mime a dog. If the children correctly identify the word you mime, show them the picture to confirm that they got it right. Continue playing until all the pictures have been used.

To make the game easier

Assign a partner to each child. Allow them to work in pairs so that they can help each other discuss and identify the word you're miming.

To make the game harder

Choose to mime a word that is a complex noun and requires the children to use higher-order thinking skills.

Clumps

This active game is a great way to get children to think about the sounds in words.

⭐ Resources

None

⭐ How to play

This game is best played in a large, open space such as the playground or gymnasium. Tell the children that you are going to play a running game. Tell them to run about the room. When they hear your signal, such as a whistle blowing, they must get into a group of four with the children closest to them. Once the children are in their groups, give them a sound such as **b**, **m**, **sh**, **th** or **j**. They must then each think of a word beginning with that sound. The first group to put their hands up and give four different words beginning with that sound wins a point. Now, instead of running individually, the children have to run around with their team. The next time they hear a signal they need to stop and generate another four words with the target sound. The game continues as explained above until a team earns five points and is declared the winner.

Depending on the size of your group, you may choose to make the teams larger or smaller.

To make the game easier

Once the children have formed their group, ask them to generate just one word that begins with the target sound.

To make the game harder

Tell the group that they must think of their four words within a time limit. For instance, you might say 'The sound is **f**. Think now. 1, 2, 3, 4, 5, stop.' Then ask the group to share their words.

Finger spelling

Children will enjoy this hands-on activity that teaches them about initial word sounds.

⭐ Resources

Pencils and paper

⭐ How to play

Give each child a pencil and a piece of paper. Tell them to place one of their hands on their paper with their fingers spread out. Now the children must draw round their hand. Give each child a letter sound to write on the palm of their hand outline, such as **f**. They then have to think of and spell or draw five things beginning with that sound, one for each finger. You can give everyone in the group the same sound, and then find out who generated the same list of words and who was able to generate different and interesting words. Alternatively, you can give each child a different sound with which to work.

After the children have generated their five words or drawings, tell them to cut out the outline of their hands and put them on display in the room.

To make the game easier

Give out pencils and paper as above so that each child can draw round their hand. As a group, generate a list of four words that begin with the target sound. Then ask the children to write or draw independently a fifth word beginning with the target sound.

To make the game harder

Ask the children to do this activity without saying the words. This requires them to rely on their phonemic knowledge of the words.

Finish it off

Through teaching the children about alliteration, they will learn to detect and generate words with the same initial sounds.

⭐ Resources

Flipchart; pen

⭐ How to play

Give the group the beginning of some alliterative sentences and ask them to think of different ways to finish them. Here are examples you can start with:

- ✪ Sally smiled sweetly at …
- ✪ Naughty Nathan …
- ✪ Terrible toys …
- ✪ Rabbits ran …

Once the children have thought about different way to complete their sentences, record their ideas on a flipchart.

To make the game easier

Write a list of words that begin with the same sound on a flipchart. Share the list with the group, and encourage them to work in pairs to string the words together to make an alliterative sentence.

To make the game harder

Encourage the children to make alliterative sentences that are more than five words long.

Let's go shopping

In this game the children will enjoy playing the role of shoppers who search for items that begin with the same sound.

⭐ Resources

Pencils and paper; pretend money

⭐ How to play

Tell the children that they are going to set up a shop. Explain that this is a special shop because it only sells things that begin with the same sound. Choose a target sound such as **f**. Ask the children to think of one thing beginning with the target sound, and tell them to draw it on their paper. You will play the role of the shop keeper and the children will come to you to see whether or not their item is sold in the shop. If the item begins with the target sound, it can be displayed in the shop area.

Once the shop is fully stocked with items, the children go shopping and buy items that start with the same sound.

This is a great way to introduce new phonemes as it provides an activity rich in just one sound. You can repeat the game the following week by changing the target phoneme and restocking the shop accordingly.

To make the game easier

Brainstorm with the group a list of items that could go in the shop, and then ask the children to draw them.

To make the game harder

Encourage the children to think creatively when deciding what item to add to the shop. For instance, if the target phoneme is **s**, a smiley face or a silly car would be acceptable.

That sound

This kinaesthetic activity is a great way to link alphabetical sounds and symbols.

⭐ Resources

None

⭐ How to play

This game is best suited to a large, open space. Divide the children into groups of two or three. Tell the children that they are going to work with their group to form a letter shape with their body that corresponds with a sound that you say. Begin the game by saying a sound in isolation, such as **f**, **p** or **m**. The children can choose either to make the letter shape individually or to work as a group to form the letter shape.

Once the children grasp the concept of this game, you can begin to say words and ask the group to form the first sound of words. For instance, the groups would form a **b** for the word **basket**, **sh** for the word **shoe**, and so on.

To make the game easier

Write the target sound on a flipchart in large print. This will assist the children in forming the letter shape with their bodies.

To make the game harder

Use multisyllabic words such as **calculator**, **elephant** and **television** to increase the complexity of the task.

Sound exchange

This game is a fun way to help children identify initial word sounds.

⭐ Resources

Pictures or items from the room that begin with a consonant (see page 134)

⭐ How to play

Tell the group that they are going to play a listening game. You are going to point to and name some items and pictures in the room. The children must identify whether the item was named correctly, and whether all the sounds were present. For instance, if when holding a pencil you say 'I've got a bencil', the children identify whether you said the word correctly and then tell you which sound was missing. They will probably be able to identify easily whether the object was named correctly. It will be more difficult for them to say which sound was missing as this requires them to isolate individual phonemes. It may be necessary for you to model how the game is played before starting it with the children.

To make the game easier

The aim is for the children to listen to your word without any reference to written letters or graphemes. However, it may helpful to begin the game by writing the incorrectly named word on a flipchart, so that the group can see what sounds need to be exchanged. On seeing the word they will be able to explain more easily the changes that need to be made to the word.

To make the game harder

Ask the children to work the sounds out before telling you what the correct pronunciation of the word is. For instance, they might say 'It should be **p** not **b**. The word is pencil.'

Sound mime

This variation of charades is a fun way for the children to explore initial word sounds.

⭐ Resources

None

⭐ How to play

Put the children into groups of four and give each group a different phoneme to remember. Ask each group to think of four words they can mime that start with their phoneme. For instance, if the group's phoneme is **b**, they could choose the words **ball**, **bird**, **bath** and **baby**. When all the groups have prepared their mimes, ask them to perform them for the other groups. The groups in the audience then have to guess the words and identify the phoneme each group was given.

You can award points to the various teams for selecting words that begin with the target phoneme, guessing the mimes and identifying the phonemes.

To make the game easier

If the groups are having a difficult time generating words that begin with their target phoneme, you can prompt them with clues. For instance, if a group's target phoneme is **h**, you might say 'I'm thinking of a large animal you can ride on, and something that grows from your head that you need to brush.'

To make the game harder

Ask each group to generate at least one word that is two syllables long and one word that is a verb.

Sounds collage

In this game the children work together to make a collage of things beginning with a target phoneme.

⭐ Resources

Old magazines; scissors; glue; paper

⭐ How to play

Assign the children to groups of three or four. Give each group a magazine, scissors, glue and a piece of paper. Also give each group a target phoneme. Ask them to look through the magazine and find pictures of things beginning with that sound. The group should then work together to find suitable pictures that they can cut out to create a collage. Once their collage is completed, ask the children to share their collages with the rest of the group.

To make the game easier

Reduce the choice of pictures given to the group by selecting certain pages from the magazine. This will help the groups identify the pictures with the target phonemes. Once the appropriate pictures have been identified, the children should create their collages as explained above.

To make the game harder

In addition to finding pictures from the magazine, ask each child in the group to draw on the collage a picture that starts with the target phoneme.

Stand up / sit down

Children will enjoy learning from their peers as they race to generate words beginning with the same sound.

⭐ Resources

None

⭐ How to play

Ask the children to sit in a circle. Say a phoneme such as **n** to one child in the circle. Each child then has a turn to think of a word beginning with that phoneme. When they have thought of their word, they must stand up. The aim is for the whole group to be standing to indicate that they've thought of a word beginning with the target sound. If a child cannot think of an appropriate word, the rest of the group can help them by giving clues. However, warn the group that the whole circle will have to sit down and start the game again if someone shouts out a word when it is not their turn.

Once the whole group is standing, choose another child and give them a different sound. That child then starts another chain of words. This time the aim for the group is for each to sit down as they say a word.

Before starting the game, you need to decide whether or not you will accept nonsense words that fit the phonemic criteria.

To make the game easier

Provide clues for children who are struggling to generate appropriate words.

To make the game harder

Tell the group that everyone must say their word and be standing (or sitting) within a time limit of, say, one to two minutes. If you play the game more than once, challenge the children to try to beat their original time record to encourage them to generate the words at a faster pace.

Time to vote

This listening game helps children discriminate between initial phonemes.

⭐ Resources

Pictures or items from the room that begin with a consonant (see page 134); pencils and paper. We have provided some pictures to help you get started. However, you may choose to extend the game with pictures from magazines, the Internet or clip art software.

⭐ How to play

Distribute a pencil and a piece of paper to each child. Tell them to draw a big cross on one side of their paper and a large tick on the other. Explain that when you name a picture or item in the room, they must signal whether you said the word in the right way or not by holding up the tick or cross.

If there are children in the group who experience difficulty with particular speech sounds, or sometimes hear the wrong sounds when attempting to spell a word, individualise this activity for them. For instance, if a child regularly mixes up the sounds **sh** and **s**, choose a group of words to say correctly and incorrectly that begin with these sounds. This will provide many opportunities for them to hear the differences.

To make the game easier

Exchange sounds that are phonetically very different. For instance, exchange long sounds such as **sh**, **f**, **s**, **m** and **n** with short sounds such as **p**, **t**, **k**, **b**, **d** and **g**. This will allow the children to discriminate more easily between the two sounds than voiced and unvoiced pairs such as **p/b**, **t/d**, **k/g** and **f/v**.

To make the game harder

Ask the children to work out the correct sounds in each word without saying them.

What am I?

This game is a great way for the children to generate vocabulary that starts with the same sound.

⭐ Resources

None

⭐ How to play

This game is best suited to an open area such as the playground or gymnasium. Put the children into groups of four. Explain to them that you are going to give each group a phoneme or sound to remember. Their task is to think of four words that start with that sound and to be ready to act them out for the other groups. For instance, if the group's sound is **b**, they might choose to mime **bat**, **birthday**, **broom** and **ball**. Each member of the group must think of and mime a different word for the rest of the children. Once the other children have worked out the first mime, it will become easier for them to work out the other mimes because they will have identified the initial sound of the words. Once a group has finished miming their four words, encourage the rest of the children to discuss what they think the initial sounds of the words were.

To make the game easier

Use picture cards with the children, so that they can concentrate on choosing an appropriate word for the target sound instead of on generating vocabulary. You could use pictures from magazines, the Internet or clip art software.

To make the game harder

Give each child in the group a different phoneme.

What's on the menu?

This game is an interactive and exciting way for the children to work with initial sounds in words.

⭐ Resources

Pencils; a piece of A4 paper for each child

⭐ How to play

Assign each child a partner and give each pair a different phoneme. Give each pair a pencil and a piece of paper. The task is to name a café and create a menu that has items of food on it that begin with their target phoneme. They can either draw or write the name of the food items. For instance, a pair whose target phoneme is **m** might have:

- ✪ mushrooms on toast;
- ✪ meatballs with spaghetti;
- ✪ monster chocolate cake;
- ✪ marshmallows on hot chocolate.

After the children have finished, ask them to tell the other groups what is on their menu. The children can listen to one another's menus and decide which café would be their favourite place to visit.

To make the game easier

Give all the children the same phoneme. Brainstorm a list of different foods that begin with that sound. Then let the pairs of children devise and design the menu, using some of the food items from the brainstorming list.

To make the game harder

Give the pairs of children two phonemes which have to appear in each food item. For instance, if a group has the phonemes **s** and **p**, they might include the following items on their menu:

- ✪ pea soup;
- ✪ super pineapples;
- ✪ sweet potatoes;
- ✪ pancakes with syrup.
- ✪ pizza with sweetcorn;

Where's my partner?

In this game the children enjoy identifying what is shown on a picture and what its initial sound is.

⭐ Resources

Pictures for half the number of children in your group (you could use those on page 134); initial phoneme cards that correspond with each of the pictures above (see page 136); sticky tape. You could also use pictures from magazines, the Internet or clip art software.

⭐ How to play

Divide the children into two groups. Using sticky tape, attach a picture to the back of each child in the first group. Distribute the corresponding phoneme cards to each of the remaining children. The children with pictures on their back are to work out what their picture is by asking the other children questions about it. Once a child has correctly identified the picture, they must find the child who has a phoneme that is the first sound in their word. If both children agree that the picture matches the first sound on the phoneme card, the pair sit down.

When all the children have been paired up and are sitting, swap the groups around and give pictures to those that had letters and vice versa. Throughout the game, encourage the group to say the possible words and to work out the initial sound of these words.

To make the game easier

Reduce the choice of initial phonemes by using only pictures that start with two or three different phonemes.

To make the game harder

Once the children find their partner, ask them to think of more words that begin with the target sound.

Who can think?

The children think of words that begin with a variety of sounds.

⭐ Resources

None

⭐ How to play

Ask the children to sit in a circle. Tell the group that you are going to play a word game. Start the game by choosing a target sound, asking the question: 'Who can think of something that begins with …?' The first child to think of a word beginning with the target sound asks the next question, choosing a different target sound. Continue playing the game until everyone has had a chance to answer and ask a question. You may consider limiting each child to answering and asking just one question per round to ensure that everyone has an equal chance to take part in the game. The game ends when all of the children have had a turn at answering and asking a question.

To make the game easier

Before starting the game, write a selection of sounds on a flipchart. This will help the children to think quickly of sounds for their questions. If the group cannot generate words purely from the initial sounds, give them some semantic clues to help them think of an appropriate word. For instance, to help a child think of a word beginning with **p**, you might say 'I can think of something beginning with **p** that you write with.'

To make the game harder

Ask the children to vary their questions as follows:

✪ 'Who can think of something ending with **s** sound?'
✪ 'Who can think of two words starting with **b** or **s**?'

Final run

This game is a fun and exciting way to teach children about final consonants in words.

⭐ Resources

Three sets of pictures for words with the same final consonant sound (see page 137); three boxes; sticky tape; marker

⭐ How to play

Set out the three boxes at one end of the room. Write three final consonants such as **p**, **t** and **l**, one on each box, with a marker. Tell the children that their task is to work out the final sound of a picture and to put their picture in the corresponding box. For instance, a cat would go in the **t** box, a cup would go in the **p** box, and so on.

Tell the children to line up at the opposite end of the room from where the boxes are. Give each child a picture. Encourage the group to say their word and work out the last sound they can hear. They must then take turns to say the final sound of the word, run to the right box, and put their picture in it. When all the pictures have been put into a box, empty the boxes with the children and say together what all the pictures show. Discuss with the group whether the pictures are in the right box. Saying the words together helps the children who are struggling to hear the similarity and repetition of the final sound. If time permits, you can play the game again, shuffling the cards and redistributing them. You could vary the game by having the children hop, jump or skip to the boxes to make it more exciting and active.

To make the game easier

Reduce the choices by using only two boxes and two final sounds. You can further simplify the game by saying the word for the child, rather than asking them to work out the final sound independently. For instance, you might say 'It's a ball. Ball. What sound can you hear at the end of the word **ball**?' If the task remains too hard, add 'Does it end with **l** or **s**?'

To make the game harder

Encourage the children to work out the final sound of the word without saying it.

An added challenge is to increase the number of boxes and pictures that you give to the group.

Suggested word list

✪ Words with final sound **g**
bag, dog, egg, flag, frog, jug, leg, mug, peg, plug, rag, rug

✪ Words with final sound **c/k**
bike, black, book, cake, clock, duck, fork, lake, neck, sock, stick

✪ Words with final sound **s**
bus, dice, dress, face, glass, grass, horse, house, mouse, nurse, police, rice

✪ Words with final sound **t**
boat, carpet, carrot, cat, coat, dart, eight, feet, gate, hat, kite, mat, net, nut, plate, rat, root, yacht

✪ Words with final sound **m**
arm, bomb, comb, cream, farm, game, jam, lamb, room, swim, thumb

✪ Words with final sound **p**
cup, pipe, rope, sheep, shop, soap, tap

Finish off

In this lively game, the children learn how to identify the final sounds in a word using picture cues and a puppet.

⭐ Resources

Puppet; pictures of words with a final consonant sound (see page 137); flipchart; pen

⭐ How to play

Introduce your puppet to the group. Explain that the puppet is very clever because they can name lots of pictures. However, the puppet sometimes forgets to say the whole word and often doesn't say the final sound.

Choose a picture to show to the children. Ask the puppet to name the picture for you. The puppet will then say the following words with the final consonant sound missing: **bu** for **bus**, **ca** for **cat**, and so on.

Ask the children to tell you what sound is missing from each of the words. Then ask the group to say the word correctly for the puppet. Invite a child to come and write the missing letter on the flipchart.

To make the game easier

Start by asking the children whether or not the puppet said the word correctly. In this instance, the puppet will have to say some of the words correctly and some incorrectly. When the puppet says a word incorrectly, ask the group a question such as 'Can anyone tell me what the sound at the end of the word should be? Busss, busss. What sound do you hear at the end of **bus**?' If the children are confused and give you other sounds in that word, accept and then refocus on the final sound: 'Yes, there is a **b** in the word **bus**. What other sound can you hear? Bus.'

To make the game harder

Ask the children to work out the final sound silently in their head. When they think they know what the missing sound is, they can put their hands up to tell you. Challenge the group further by asking them if they can think of any other words ending in that sound.

Odd one out

This game is an entertaining way to help children discriminate between different sounds in words.

⭐ Resources

Pairs of pictures with the same final sound (see page 138); sticky tape

⭐ How to play

Stick up three pictures for the children to see. Name the pictures with them. Tell them that the focus of today's game is to work out the sounds at the ends of words. You are going to say three words and their task is to work out which word doesn't belong. For instance, you might say 'Cat, bus, meat. Which word is the odd one out?'

The team that answers correctly gets a point. Continue playing in this way.

To make the game easier

For children who find this difficult, think about the distracters you use. For instance, the following pairings are easier because they sound very different: **t** and **m**, **k** and **f** and **d** and **sh**.

Another way to simplify the game is to display only one picture at a time and work with the group to decide on the final sound of the word. When the group has done that, invite a child to write the final sound underneath the picture using a sticky note. Continue in this manner until the final sound of the third picture has been worked out. Then discuss which picture is the odd one out and why.

To make the game harder

Choose distracters that are harder to discriminate between, such as **p** and **b**, **t** and **k**, **s** and **sh**, and **m** and **n**.

Pack away

This enjoyable game uses props to teach final sounds in words.

✪ Resources

Suitcase and selection of holiday items that end in a consonant

✪ How to play

Give each child an item for the suitcase. Ask each to name their item. As they do this, they must also work out the last sound of their word. The children might say 'Brush ends with sh' or 'Hat ends in t.'

Tell the children that they are going to help pack your suitcase, but that you're going to start with things that end with **k**. Encourage them to recall the last sound of their item and to offer it to you if it ends with the target sound. Repeat with a new target sound, and continue playing in this manner until every child has packed their item.

To make the game easier

Say the words with the children and break them down into phonemes, such as **br u sh**, to help them identify the final sound in each.

To make the game harder

Ask the group to work out the final sound of the item in their head. Give each child more than one item to pack.

Suggested items to pack in the suitcase

- ✪ spade
- ✪ sock
- ✪ sun cream
- ✪ hat
- ✪ book
- ✪ cash

- ✪ chocolate
- ✪ trainers (final sound z)
- ✪ sun glasses (final sound z)
- ✪ swimming costume
- ✪ ticket
- ✪ pen

- ✪ shirt
- ✪ pyjamas (final sound z)
- ✪ passport
- ✪ doll
- ✪ sandals (final sound z)
- ✪ phone

Swap it

This hands-on game is a great way to teach segmenting and blending.

⭐ Resources

Selection of consonant cards from the phoneme cards (see page 136); flipchart; sticky tape

⭐ How to play

Give each child a phoneme card from the list below. On the flipchart write a consonant–vowel combination such as **pa**. Tell each child to look at their card and to determine whether or not their phoneme could be added to the end of **pa** to make a real word. For instance, a child with a **t** on their phoneme card could make the word **pat**, while a child with the phoneme **f** could not make a real word. If there is a child with a phoneme such as **k** that could be added to **pa** to make **pack**, explain that **pack** is indeed a real word, but that it is spelled p-a-c-k. Using sticky tape, invite the children to come and stick their phoneme card onto the end of the consonant–vowel combination to demonstrate the blending of the sounds.

To make the game easier

Write a consonant–vowel combination on the flipchart as explained above. Instead of distributing a phoneme card to each child, put the phonemes in a pile next to the flipchart. Pick up a card and stick it next to the consonant–vowel combination. As a group, decide what the consonant–vowel–consonant combination would say and whether or not it would make a real word. After doing this as a group a couple of times, invite a few children to come forward and stick the phoneme card onto the flipchart. Ask them if they can determine whether the card they've stuck to the flipchart makes it a real word.

Help the group with the blending task by exaggerating the sounds in a word. Do not say the word by its letter names, nor just by disjointed letter sounds, but rather blend the sounds like this: mmmaaann.

To make the game harder

Tell the children to blend the sound of the word in their head. Ask them not to say the word until they are sure they know what it is.

Suggested list for phoneme cards: p, b, m, n, t, d, f, s, sh, ch, j, k, g, ll

Harder selection for phoneme cards: as above, plus th, z, x, v, st

Dot to dot

This hands-on game is a unique way to teach children how to listen for final sounds.

⭐ Resources

Dot-to-dot page (see page 139)

⭐ How to play

Give each child a pencil and a dot-to-dot page. Tell the group that two dots can only be joined if they hear a particular sound. The sounds they should be listening for are at the end of words. If, for instance, your target sound is **s**, you might say **class**. The children must then decide whether or not they heard an **s** at the end of the word. Encourage the children to say the word in order to isolate the final sound. If there was an **s**, the group then joins a dot to a dot on their page. If they did not hear a word with the final target sound, they do nothing. Take advantage of the fact that pictures are not needed for this activity and include words which are not nouns, such as **yes**, **less**, **this** and **plus**. The activity continues until the children have been able to form an interesting design on their paper.

To make the game easier

Think carefully about the words you use as distracters. If the group is listening for **s** at the end of words, **sh** and **f** are harder to discriminate between than **m**, **b** or **k**.

To make the game harder

Use polysyllabic words with the group. This will be more difficult because there will be more sounds for the children to discriminate between.

May I come in?

In this active game the children must find words with a final target sound.

⭐ Resources

None

⭐ How to play

Tell the children to form a queue. Select two of the children to form an arch through which the rest can pass. These two children form the arch by raising their hands and then joining them. Tell the children that the task today is to work out the sounds at the ends of words. The children forming the arch decide upon a target phoneme. One by one the children approach the arch and ask, for example, 'Please may I come in? My word is **man**.' If their word ends with the target phoneme the arch has chosen, the child may pass through it. If the last sound in the child's word does not have the target phoneme, then the arch gently comes down on the child's head and that child must go to the end of the queue.

It may be necessary to demonstrate the game with a few words to get them familiar with the logistics of the game.

To make the game easier

Simplify the game by selecting a final target phoneme as a group. Then generate some words with the target sound before starting the game.

To make the game harder

When the arch collapses on a child's head, the children forming the arch must change their target phoneme.

Cross it off

This simple task is a great way to teach children how to listen for final sounds in words.

★ Resources

Pencils and paper

★ How to play

Give each child a pencil and paper. Tell them to write down the following consonants and digraphs: p, b, t, d, ck, g, l, m, n, s, sh, f, th and z. The purpose of the game is for the children to listen to the word you say and determine the last sound in it. They must then find the corresponding consonant or digraph and cross it out. For example, if your word is **goat**, the children must find the letter **t** on their paper and cross it out. Continue playing the game until all the letters have been crossed out.

Encourage the children to say the word and work out the final sound by segmenting it into chunks. For instance, **red** becomes re-d, **name** becomes na-me, and so on. Because pictures are not needed for the game, take the opportunity to use words that are not nouns.

To make the game easier

You can simplify the game by allowing the children to work in pairs. When working in pairs they are more likely to say and hear the sounds with which they are working than if they were working independently. The game is also easier if you restrict the number of sounds the children are listening for. You may consider starting with just four different phonemes but have each one written two or three times on the paper, so that there are several opportunities to hear the sound in different words.

You could also do this as a whole-group activity and have the letters written on a flipchart. When you say the word the entire group works it out, and one child is selected to cross it off the flipchart.

To make the game harder

Ask the children to work out the final sound of the word without saying it.

Sort me out

In this game the children identify the final sound in an item pictured.

⭐ Resources

Pictures of words that end with one of three consonant sounds (see page 140); consonant phoneme cards (see page 136)

⭐ How to play

Distribute the pictures to all but three children. Ask those three to stand at the front. Give each one of them a consonant phoneme card.

The aim is for the children to identify the last sound in their picture. They must then give it to one of the three at the front. For instance, if those at the front are collecting words ending in **s**, **d** or **p**, a child with a picture of a map would work out the final sound, and give it to the child collecting words ending in **p**. The latter has to judge whether or not they have been given a picture that ends with their target sound.

The game continues until all the pictures have been sorted between the three children. Then ask those three to name all of the pictures they have collected. This reinforces the final sound of the words to the rest of the group.

To make the game easier

Start the game by choosing two final sounds. Give the pictures to pairs of children so they can work together.

To make the game harder

Instead of using pictures, tell the rest of the children to think of a word that ends with one of the target sounds. They should say it to the appropriate child at the front, who decides whether it ends with their target sound. Continue until each child has had a chance to say a word.

What's at the end?

This active game is an enjoyable way for children to listen for final sounds in words.

⭐ Resources

Consonant cards; sticky tape

⭐ How to play

Tape a different consonant card on each of the four walls of the room where they can be seen by the children. Tell the group that they are going to play a listening game. Their task is to listen for the last sound in the words you say. When they hear the last sound, they must run to the wall with the corresponding final consonant. You can vary the game by telling the children to move like different animals, such as a snake, elephant or monkey.

To make the game easier

Simplify the game by using only two consonant cards at first. You can also start by using nonsense vowel–consonant combinations such as **ap**, **im**, **ug**, and so on.

To make the game harder

Choose multisyllabic words to add to the level of difficulty. You may even decide to select some children to choose the words to tell the rest of the group.

Final draw

Working in pairs, the children will help one another to work out the final sound in various drawings.

⭐ Resources

Pencils and paper

⭐ How to play

Put the children in pairs and hand out a pencil and paper to each pair. Give each a different final consonant such as p, b, t, d, g, ck, m, n, ll, sh, s or f.

Tell the children to write their letter or letters on the piece of paper. They must then think of something to draw that ends with the final consonant you gave them. For instance, if a pair has the letter **p**, they could draw a small picture of a sheep. When all pairs have finished their pictures, tell the children to pass their papers to another group so everyone in the room has swapped papers. The first thing each pair must do is work out the final sound of the picture on the paper that has been given to them. They must then check that the last sound in the picture corresponds to the letter that is written on the paper. The pairs then think of a different word that ends in that sound, such as **mop**, and draw it on the paper. When the drawing is completed, all groups swap papers again with a different pair, and the game continues until all the groups have drawn on every paper. If you are working with a particularly large group, you may decide to reduce the number of times the papers are swapped. Encourage the children to say their words out loud and to listen to their partner to ensure that their word has the final target sound.

To make the game easier

Before telling the group to swap their papers with another pair, ask the children to check with you that what they drew ends with the target sound.

To make the game harder

Ask each group to think of and draw more than one thing that ends with the target sound. Alternatively, you could have the children work independently instead of in pairs so that they are relying on their own phonic abilities.

Find your group

The children will enjoy working with others to work out final sounds in words.

⭐ Resources

Two sets of pictures with the same final sound (page 138). Depending on the size of your group, you may need as few as two pictures with the same final sound. If you are working with a larger group, you'll need larger sets of pictures that end with the same sound.

⭐ How to play

Give a picture card to each child. Tell the group that they must find other children in the group who have a picture of something that ends with the same sound as their picture. For instance, if a child has a picture of a frog, they must work out the last sound in their word and then find other children who have a picture whose last sound is **g**. The game ends when all of the children have found the group to which they belong.

Once all of the children have found their group, ask them to hold up and name their pictures for the rest of the group. This provides valuable auditory feedback about the final sound. Encourage the children to say the words and to listen to others in their group to check that they have identified the final sound correctly.

To make the game easier

Reduce the number of final sounds in the sets of pictures distributed to the group.

To make the game harder

Once the children have found their group, ask them to think of five more words that end with that sound.

Thumbs up

This game is a simple way to teach final sound recognition in words.

⭐ Resources

None

⭐ How to play

This is a quick and easy game for filling a few minutes. Tell the group that they are going to play a listening game. If they agree with what you say, they are to put their thumbs up. If they disagree with what you say, they are to put their thumbs down. Start the game by saying 'Sock ends with the sound k.' The children must then indicate with their thumbs whether or not they agree with your statement. Continue making true and false statements until you've worked through a range of phonetic sounds with which the group is familiar.

To make the game easier

Give children who are less confident the option of putting their thumb out horizontally, to indicate that they're not sure. Encourage the children to say the words as this gives them the chance to hear the sounds again.

To make the game harder

Choose words with more syllables to add to the level of difficulty. In addition, encourage the children not to say the word so that they have to rely on their internal knowledge of phonics. Alternatively, choose some of the children to generate the words and the true or false statement for the group. In this instance, the remainder of the group would continue playing as explained above, signalling with thumbs to show their agreement or disagreement.

Snap

The children play Snap to help them identify final sounds.

⭐ Resources

Two sets of pictures that end with the same final sound (page 138). We have provided some pictures to help you get started. However, you may choose to extend the game with pictures from magazines, the Internet or clip art software.

⭐ How to play

Put the children into pairs. Divide the sets of pictures evenly amongst the pairs. Tell the children that they'll be playing a variation of the game Snap. When they flip over their picture cards, they must name their picture and identify the final sound in the word. The children can only call out 'Snap' if the two cards turned over both end with the same sound. The first child in the pair to call 'Snap' wins their partner's pile of used cards. The game continues until all of the pictures have been used up.

To make the game easier

Go through the cards before you start the game and talk about the final sounds. Draw attention to the fact that some of the words end with the same sound.

To make the game harder

When a child wins a pile of cards, challenge them to think of another word that ends with the same sound.

What's my word?

This fast-paced game is a great way to practise blending phonemes at the end of words.

⭐ Resources

None

⭐ How to play

Before starting the game choose a consonant–vowel combination that you'd like the children to practise with, such as **ca** or **sa**. Start the game by saying, for example, 'I'm thinking of a word and it starts with **sa**.' The children then have to suggest a final sound that could complete the word. For instance, they might suggest **t** for **sat**, **p** for **sap** or **k** for **sack**.

If a child suggests a nonsense word but has correctly blended the phonemes together, praise them for their effort and suggest some final sounds which would change the word into a real word. If a child says a word but has changed the original consonant–vowel combination, draw their attention to what they have changed and encourage them to try again.

To make the game easier

After choosing your consonant–vowel combination, write some phonemes that could complete your word on a flipchart. Ask the children to try to make a word by adding a final sound to the end of your consonant–vowel combination.

To make the game harder

Until the children have thought of a word, challenge them to blend the sounds together without saying them. Once they have thought of their word, they can put their hand up and say it for you.

What's my sound?

In this game the children work independently in groups to determine the final sounds in words.

⭐ Resources

Phoneme cards (see page 136)

⭐ How to play

Give each child a consonant phoneme card and tell them to stand in a circle. Explain to the group that you're going to play a listening game. When you say a word, the children must listen for their sound at the end. If they hear their sound they must sit down. For instance, if you say **dog**, any child who has the phoneme card with **g** on it must sit down. Continue playing the game in this manner until all the children have sat down. Keep in mind that there are no pictures needed for this game and you can therefore use words that are not nouns in order to extend the vocabulary with which the children are working.

To make the game easier

Depending on the number of children in your group, you could put them into teams. Give each child in the group the same phoneme card. When you say a word, the group decides whether or not the word you said ends with their target sound. If the word ends with the target sound, one child from the group sits down. The first group with all of its members sitting is the winning team.

To make the game harder

Choose words with more syllables to add to the level of difficulty. Alternatively, choose some children to generate the words for the group and to decide whether the right child has sat down.

Guessing game

This fun adaptation of charades is a great way to teach children about final sounds in words.

⭐ Resources

Pictures from magazines, the Internet or clip art software

⭐ How to play

Tell the children that you are going to mime a picture and they must guess what it is. For instance, start by giving the group a phonic clue such as 'It ends with **sh**' and then mime a fish. If the children correctly identify the word you mime, show them the picture to confirm that they got it right. Continue playing until all the pictures have been used.

To make the game easier

Allow the children to work in pairs so that they can help each other discuss and identify the word you're miming.

To make the game harder

Choose a word to mime that is a complex noun and requires the children to use higher-order thinking skills.

Pair up

Children will enjoy searching for pairs of objects that end with the same sound.

★ Resources

Pictures of pairs of things that end with the same sound (see page 138).
You could also use pictures from magazines, the Internet or clip art software.

★ How to play

Tell the children to sit in a circle. Place all the pairs of objects in the circle.
Name each one to ensure that the children can identify each item correctly
and refer to it by its proper name. Choose one child from the group to find
two items that end with the same sound. Encourage the child to say the
names of the items as they search for the pair of objects. Ask them to tell
you what sound each item ends with as they handle the objects. When the
child selects the two items that they think end with the same sound, the rest
of the group say whether or not they agree. If they agree, they put their thumbs
up. If they disagree, their hands stay in their laps.

To make the game easier

As the child handles the objects, say the name of each one in a loud, clear
voice. It may be necessary to exaggerate the final sound of each word. For
instance, **man** becomes mannnn, **table** becomes tablllle and so on. To simplify
the game further, display only one half of each pair in the circle. The other
halves of the pairs should be in a neat pile in front of you. The child chooses
one of the items in front of you, and works out the final sound of that
word. Next, the child looks at the items in the circle and decides which one
ends with the same sound.

To make the game harder

Do not name the objects in the circle before starting the game. This forces the group to rely on their own knowledge of sounds and vocabulary. Choose items whose final phonemes sound similar. For instance, choosing between pairs of items that end with **b**, **m**, **k** and **sh** is a much easier selection task than choosing between pairs of items that end with **s**, **f**, **sh** and **ch**.

Suggested items for an easier game

- ✪ pen – man
- ✪ sock – cake
- ✪ mug – log
- ✪ ball – hill
- ✪ cat – boat
- ✪ cup – tap

Suggested items for a harder game

- ✪ sledge – badge
- ✪ fruit – foot
- ✪ van – violin
- ✪ watch – torch
- ✪ bus – mouse
- ✪ fish – brush
- ✪ leaf – knife

Matching pairs

This memory game will improve the children's understanding of final word sounds.

⭐ Resources

An even number of paired picture cards that end with the same sound – for instance, six cards ending with **t**, six cards ending with **m**, six cards ending with **l** (see page 140 for some examples). We have provided some pictures to help you get started. However, you may choose to extend the game with pictures from magazines, the Internet or clip art software.

⭐ How to play

Ask the children to sit in a circle. Spread out all the cards face down in the centre of the circle. Tell the group that they will have a turn to flip over two cards. They must then name the pictures and say the last sound of each word. For instance, if the child turns over a picture of a cat and a man, they would say, 'I've got **cat** and **man**. **Cat** ends with **t** and **man** ends with **n**.' If the two pictures end with the same sound the child keeps the pair, if they do not end with the same sound they are returned face down to the centre of the circle. The next child takes a turn and repeats the game play as explained above. The game continues until each card has been paired up with another that shares the same final sound.

Depending on the size of your group, a small number of children could be chosen to turn over two cards each day until the entire group has had an opportunity to participate in the game.

To make the game easier

Reduce the number of final word sounds the children work with. For instance, only put picture cards ending with **t** and **b** in the centre of the circle. This simplifies the task so that children are differentiating between two sounds only. Encourage the children to sound the words out and to help one another work out the final sound.

To make the game harder

Increase the number of final sounds the children work with. An additional challenge is to play the game with only two picture cards per sound, giving the children more opportunities to discriminate between the final sounds in words.

Possible word list

- l: ball, bell, till, sail, wheel, tail, snail, doll
- n: sweetcorn, pumpkin, man, van, wine, ten, fan, pin
- t: carrot, hat, rat, eight, rabbit, peanut, parrot, pilot
- p: lollipop, lamp, hip, bump, cap, lap, mop, map
- m: ham, lamb, mum, pram, stem, thumb, arm
- d: cloud, head, bed, sad, shed, crowd
- s: dress, horse, ice, nurse, police, bus, grass

All change

This active game encourages children to listen for final sounds independently.

⭐ Resources

None

⭐ How to play

Tell the children that they will be playing a listening game. Ask them to arrange their chairs into a large circle. Tell each child in the group one sound to remember, such as **p**, **f**, **sh** or **k**. Use up to four sounds, depending on the size of the group. One child goes to the middle of the circle and their chair is removed. Say one of the sounds. The group of children with that sound must leave their seats and find another place to sit. The child in the middle must try to sit in a vacant seat too. The child who cannot find a chair then takes a turn in the middle. The game is repeated until everyone has had a number of opportunities to swap seats.

To make the game easier

Give each child a card with a sound on it. After saying the sound, show the corresponding letter on a card. The group of children with that sound then play the game as explained above.

To make the game harder

Start the game by saying individual target sounds. Then extend the game by saying whole words that end with each of the target sounds, such as **stop**, **puff**, **fish** and **pack**.

Mr Rhyme

Children will improve their recognition of rhyming words while helping the puppet Mr Rhyme search for words.

⭐ Resources

Puppet; selection of items or pictures

⭐ How to play

Introduce the group to your puppet called Mr Rhyme. Explain to them that Mr Rhyme loves to make rhyming words. However, he loves rhyming so much that he sometimes can't say the right word. He hopes the children will be able to help him.

Choose a picture of a clock. Have Mr Rhyme point to the clock and say 'Mock'. Can the children tell him what the word should really be? Once the group understands how they're supposed to help Mr Rhyme, choose ten items or pictures and place them where they are visible to the group. Tell them that Mr Rhyme is going to say one of the words and that you'll need volunteers to work out which word he is trying to say. For instance, if Mr Rhyme says 'Mee', the child should point to the tree. Continue playing until all the items have been correctly identified.

To make the game easier

Reduce the number of items to two, if necessary. It might be helpful to say something such as 'Tree and duck, which one rhymes with mee? Tree–mee, or duck–mee?' so the group can hear the similarities and differences in the words.

To make the game harder

Once the child has identified the item Mr Rhyme was trying to say, ask them if they can think of other words that rhyme with it. Make clear to the group whether nonsense words will be accepted.

Rhyme time

In this game the children use visual cues to help them find rhyming pairs of words.

⭐ Resources

Pictures (see page 141). We have provided some pictures to help you get started. However, you may choose to extend the game with pictures from magazines, the Internet or clip art software.

⭐ How to play

Display a set of pictures to the group. Tell them that you're going to play a rhyming game together. You could say something like 'I hear with my little ear something rhyming with **dish**.' Choose one child to find a picture that rhymes with the word **dish**. Once they have chosen the correct item, ask them to say the two words together to reinforce the concept of rhyme. To indicate their agreement with the child's answer, the rest of the group could put their thumbs up. If the group don't agree, their hands stay on their laps. If the child is correct, they keep the picture.

You can decide whether you'd like to allow nonsense words for the purposes of this game.

To make the game easier

Reduce the number of items displayed. After you have said the rhyming word, start listing other rhyming words. This helps the child hear the word being segmented and the initial sound being changed.

To make the game harder

To make this game more challenging, do not provide any visual cues for the group. Instead, ask the child to find an object in the room that rhymes with the word you said. To demonstrate this concept, you might say 'I hear with my little ear something rhyming with **poor**.' The child could then respond with a rhyming word such as **floor** or **door**.

Clap rhyme

In this game the children compete in pairs to be the first one to find a rhyming word.

⭐ Resources

None

⭐ How to play

Arrange the children in a line. Choose two children to stand face to face with one another. Say a word and tell the children to clap their hands once and say another word that rhymes with the word you gave them. The first child from the pair to say a rhyming word correctly remains standing. The other child returns to the end of the line. The next child in line stands face to face with the child who has just won and the game continues as before. This continues until all children have had a turn. Depending on the size of your group, you may want to play this game each day with smaller numbers, until everyone has had a chance to participate.

You can decide whether to accept nonsense words for the purposes of this game.

To make the game easier

As a group, generate a few rhyming words for your target word before starting the game. Then select two children to face each other. Give them the target word and see who can clap their hands and generate a rhyming word first.

To make the game harder

Ask the children to say two or more rhyming words after they clap.

Rhyming hoops

This active game is a great way to teach children how to generate rhyming words.

⭐ Resources

Hoops

⭐ How to play

In an open area of the room, place three hoops in front of each group of four to six children. Depending on the number of children you're working with, you may need to make the groups bigger or smaller. Tell the children that they are going to practise rhyming words today. They will take turns jumping through a hoop for each rhyming word they think of. Their target is to generate three rhyming words so that they can get to the end of the hoops. You can demonstrate this game by saying 'I can think of three words that rhyme with **day: say, may, hay**' as you jump through the hoops. Give the first child a consonant–vowel–consonant or consonant–vowel word. See the next page for some suggested words. The remainder of the group can show their agreement with the child's words by putting their thumbs up.

If you're working with a particularly large group of children, you could pair the children for this game. They could hold hands as they jump through the hoops and say the words together. Alternatively, individual children could be chosen each day until the entire group has participated in the game.

To make the game easier

If the child is finding it difficult to generate rhyming words, you could give them some prompts such as 'Words rhyming with **car**? Try **f**. Can you make a rhyming word with **f**? Car–far.'

You could make the task even simpler by changing the game into a rhyme detection task. For example, you would say two words and ask the child to tell you whether or not they rhyme. If the words do rhyme, the child repeats the two words and jumps through one hoop. At the next hoop ask the child to generate a rhyme with the target sound. If they still cannot think of a word, repeat a rhyme detection task as above.

To make the game harder

Ask the child to generate five rhymes from the word you generated. You could display all the consonant phonemes on cards to assist them with this more challenging task.

Suggested words

✪ tea	✪ moo	✪ car	✪ four	✪ hi
✪ man	✪ ball	✪ pick	✪ go	✪ pay
✪ cat	✪ leg	✪ tap		

Guess my picture

Children will enjoy working in teams to work out your secret rhyming word.

⭐ Resources

Flipchart; pen

⭐ How to play

Divide the class into two teams. Give the children a rhyming clue for the picture you are about to draw. For instance, if you are going to draw a picture of a tree, you might say 'Key'. As you begin drawing your picture on the flipchart, the children from both teams should raise their hands if they think they can guess what you are drawing before you have finished the picture.

Award one point to the team for each word they generate that rhymes with your word, even if it isn't correct. Award two points to the first team to guess the word correctly. Continue playing with different words until a team earns ten points.

If you find it difficult to keep score and draw at the same time, you can appoint a child from each team to keep track of their team's score.

To make the game easier

Repeat the rhyming clue for your picture several times before starting your drawing. Then encourage the group to generate some rhyming words from your clue. This will guide them to the target word.

To make the game harder

To make the children focus on the rhyming element of this game, deduct points for words that are suggested but do not rhyme with your clue.

Monster names

Children will enjoy creating original artwork while generating rhymes.

⭐ Resources

Paper; coloured pencils or crayons

⭐ How to play

This is a short, fun game that will only take about five to ten minutes. Distribute a piece of paper and coloured pencils or crayons to each child. Ask the group to draw a funny-looking monster on their paper – the more peculiar, the better. Then ask them to name their monster. The catch is that the name must rhyme – for instance, Funky Wunky, Lubby Hubby, Sloppy Poppy. The children will enjoy making these silly rhymes and deciding which one best suits their picture.

To make the game easier

Give the children some descriptive words to help them think of a monster name. Here are some suggestions:

✪ fussy	✪ silly	✪ odd	✪ dusty
✪ mucky	✪ dirty	✪ shy	✪ slimy
✪ messy	✪ lumpy	✪ grimy	✪ slippery.

To make the game harder

See if the children can make up a rhyming first, middle and surname for their monster, such as Jammy Whammy Sammy.

Rhyming names

Children will enjoy making rhyming sentences with their names in this game.

⭐ Resources

Paper and pencils

⭐ How to play

Tell the children that you are going to make rhymes with everyone's name. For instance:

- ✪ Mel learns to spell.
- ✪ Lee likes tea.
- ✪ Zac loves to quack.
- ✪ Peter is a meter.

It might be helpful to create some silly pictures showing these rhyming pairs.

Select one name from the group and see if the children can think of a rhyming description. There may be several ideas. The person whose name you rhyme should be allowed to choose the one they like the best. If no ideas are forthcoming, or the suggestions do not rhyme, you will need to start prompting the rhyme by saying something such as 'Let's make some words that rhyme with Mary. Some of them will be silly words and some of them will be real words. Parey, fairy, hairy, dairy, scary …'

It is important that the group understands that rhyming words are not always spelt the same way, and that they may not be real words in English. After the rhymes have been produced, ask the children to generate a rhyme for their own name. Once this has been done, ask them to think of a rhyming term for their name. Ask the group to draw the sentence for their name.

To make the game easier

If the group is having difficulty generating words that rhyme, you can change the game into a rhyme-detection task. Choose a name and start saying words, some that rhyme and some that don't. The children must indicate if the words rhyme by raising their hand. When a rhyming pair is recognised, ask the children to say the pair of words. This helps to provide them with auditory feedback. Once the group can detect rhyme more easily, play the game as explained above.

To make the game harder

See if the group can generate several rhyming words to make a longer sentence such as 'Scary Mary likes hairy fairies.' This may require some modelling from you.

Magic spells

By creating their own magic spells, the children will increase their rhyming knowledge.

✪ Resources

Flipchart; pencils and paper

✪ How to play

Write some of the magic spells listed below on a flipchart:

- ✪ Hubble, bubble, toil and trouble
- ✪ One, two, three, turn into a tree
- ✪ Razzle, dazzle, shazzle and bazzle
- ✪ Hocus, pocus
- ✪ Hi, ho, off you go
- ✪ Abracadabra.

Read the magic spells to the children and ask them if they can hear the rhyming words. Invite some volunteers to come up to the flipchart and underline the rhyming words in each spell.

Tell the children that they are going to work in pairs to write a magic spell. They can illustrate them to make a magic rhyming display.

To make the game easier

Give the children the start of a spell. See the suggested list below.

- ✪ Nasty and mean …
- ✪ Big and tall …
- ✪ Small and sly …
- ✪ Happy or sad …
- ✪ Snakes and smoke …
- ✪ Clouds of rain …

Write the spell together as a group. Repeat the spell a couple of times with the group to reinforce the concept of rhyme.

To make the game harder

Ask the children to try to write a spell that's more than one line and has a specified minimum number of rhyming words.

Musical rhyme

This interactive game is a great way to improve children's rhyming skills.

⭐ Resources

Music CD; CD player; soft ball or beanbag

⭐ How to play

Arrange the children in a circle. Tell the group that you're going to play a rhyming game. Say a word that rhymes with a lot of other words and tell the group that they must remember your word. When you start the music, the children must pass the ball around the circle. When the music stops, the child holding the ball has to think of a word that rhymes with the word you said at the beginning of the game. The word the child says does not have to be a real word, but it must rhyme with your target word. After six turns with the target word, change the target word. Depending on the size of your group, you may want to increase or decrease the number of turns with each target word.

To make the game easier

Before starting the game, ask the group to generate some words that rhyme with the target word. Once the children are more confident with rhyming, they should be able to play the game as explained above with greater ease.

To make the game harder

Ask the child who has to generate the rhyming word to do so in a limited amount of time – say, by the time you count to 3.

Nursery rhyme time

The children will learn about rhyming pairs by listening to nursery rhymes.

⭐ Resources

Book of nursery rhymes; flipchart; pen. You can get a complete list of Mother Goose's nursery rhymes from the Internet.

⭐ How to play

Read a couple of nursery rhymes to the children. Find one that the majority of the group is familiar with. Read it slowly and deliberately. Ask the children if they can hear rhyming pairs.

As you continue reading, encourage them to try to guess the rhyming pairs before you finish reading them. For instance, 'Hickory dickory dock. The mouse ran up the …' You may want to write the rhyming pairs on a flipchart to help the group determine which nursery rhyme has the most rhyming pairs.

To make the game easier

Write several nursery rhymes on a flipchart. Read them together as a group, and then ask for volunteers to circle the rhyming pairs.

To make the game harder

Write a few of the nursery rhymes on a flipchart. After finding the rhyming words in the nursery rhyme, challenge the group to see if they can change some of the words in the nursery rhyme so that it still makes sense. For instance:

Jack and Bill
Went up the hill
To fetch a pail of water
Jack fell down
It made him brown
And Bill hid from his daughter.

Rhyming circle

This game is a fun way to help the children develop their rhyming knowledge.

✪ Resources

Flipchart; pen

✪ How to play

Ask the children to sit in a circle. Tell them you are going to make up some silly rhymes. Ask each child to choose an animal and make up a rhyme. Record these sentences on the flipchart. For instance:

- ✪ I am a fish who lives in a dish.
- ✪ I am a funny bunny.
- ✪ I am a camel, a big, shaggy mammal.
- ✪ I am a rat who won't eat that hat.

If the child's attempt does not rhyme, ask the other children to help them think of some words that do rhyme with the animal. The child can choose which word to use.

To make the game easier

Make the silly sentences together with the group, using a list of the animals and words that rhyme with them, such as:

- ✪ bird: heard, curd, third, word
- ✪ dog: log, bog, hog, fog, jog
- ✪ bear: fair, tear, chair, mare, pear
- ✪ snake: lake, bake, take, cake, shake.

To make the game harder

Ask the children to make their silly sentence silently, thus relying on internal knowledge of the words and their rhyming properties. Then choose some children to share them with the group.

Rhyme swap

This active game is a great way to reinforce the children's rhyming knowledge.

⭐ Resources

None

⭐ How to play

Arrange the children in a circle. Tell each child a word that they must remember. You can choose from the list on the next page, or use your own words that tie in with vocabulary or phonemes with which you are currently working. When telling the children their words, ensure that there are at least three other children with words from the same word family (a word family is a group of words that rhyme). Before starting the game, go round the group and check that everybody remembers their word.

Begin the game by saying a word that rhymes with one of the word families. Tell all the children who have a word that rhymes with your word to swap places. For instance, if you said **egg**, children with words such as **leg, peg** and **beg** would change places with one another. Keep in mind that you can use nonsense words as long as they rhyme with the word families the children have been given. Encourage the children to say your word and their word to check that both of the words rhyme and belong to the same word family.

You can make the game more competitive by asking one child to sit in the middle of the circle. This creates one less space in the circle so there are not enough spaces for all the children to sit down. When you call a word, the children who have a word that rhymes with yours must swap places while the child in the middle tries to get a seat. The child who is not able to get a seat then goes to the middle of the circle. They try to get a seat the next time you say a target word.

To make the game easier

When you give the children their words, give them a picture of the word to hold onto. This will help them remember their word. You can also ask the group to think of some rhyming words and nonsense words that belong to each word family before starting the game.

To make the game harder

Ask the children not to say the pair of rhyming words together, but instead to work out the rhyme in their head.

Suggested word families

✪ cat, mat, fat, hat, rat, sat, pat
✪ head, bed, said, red, shed, fed
✪ fly, shy, buy, try, my, why, pry
✪ mash, bash, lash, cash, trash

✪ leg, peg, Meg, egg, beg
✪ ball, hall, call, tall, wall, fall
✪ cap, tap, map, lap, rap, sap
✪ van, man, can, tan, pan, fan

Rhyming poems

This game helps improve children's rhyming skills while teaching them how to write a simple poem.

⭐ Resources

Flipchart; paper and pencils

⭐ How to play

Choose a simple word for which you can generate lots of rhyming words, such as **cat**. Ask the group to help you think of rhyming words for the target word and record them on a flipchart. Work together to make a poem with as many of those rhyming words as possible. For example:

✪ The cat on the mat sat on a rat, and got very fat.

✪ The rat had a bat to pat the fat cat, who sat on the mat that day.

Then ask the children to write their own poems with the rhyming words. When they have finished, choose a few children to read their poem to the rest of the group. If there is time available, the group can illustrate the poems and make a rhyming display.

It may be necessary to have a discussion about the difference between how a word is spelt and what a word sounds like. For instance, two words spelt in a similar way may not rhyme, and words spelt very differently may rhyme.

To make the game easier

Ask the children to make a clause or sentence with at least two rhyming words in it. For instance, 'The cat had a hat' or 'I sat on a mat.'

To make the game harder

Ask the children to write their own poems with a different word from the one which you practised together. Ask them to generate their own list of rhyming words and then to try to include them in a poem.

Rhyming riddles

This game is a great way to improve children's listening and rhyming skills.

⭐ Resources

Flipchart; pencils and paper

⭐ How to play

Distribute a pencil and piece of paper to each child. Alternatively, you could use whiteboards and dry erase markers for this activity. Begin the game by drawing something such as a frog on the flipchart. Make sure that the drawing is not visible to the group. Say a riddle like 'I rhyme with dog and I love to croak.' Choose one child from the group to guess what you have drawn on the flipchart, based on the riddle. Once the group understand how this game is played, assign each child a partner. Each child must think of an item to draw on their piece of paper without showing it to their partner. They must then give a rhyming clue and a semantic clue to help their partner work out what they've drawn.

To make the game easier

Instead of breaking the children into pairs to play this game, continue playing it as a group activity. Each time you play, invite a child to take a turn drawing a picture on the flipchart. Help the child think of a riddle by prompting them with questions such as these:

- ✪ Where would you find it?
- ✪ What does it look like?
- ✪ What do you do with it?
- ✪ What does it do?

To make the game harder

When the child tries to solve the riddle, ask them to do so within a time limit such as one minute.

Sit down!

This game is a fun way to teach children how to recognise rhyming words.

⭐ Resources

None

⭐ How to play

Ask the group to stand up. Tell them that they should sit down only when they hear a word that rhymes with their own name. For instance, you might say 'back' for Jack, 'fajita' for Lajita and 'lick' for Mick.

You will probably need to use nonsense words for this activity. Encourage the children to repeat the word you have said and then to say their own name. Do the two words rhyme? Continue playing the game until all the children have sat down.

To make the game easier

Let the group help one another as they hear you say the words. If the children find this difficult, then try producing a string of words that rhyme with the child's name – for instance 'Sat, flat, mat, chat, hat; whose name could it be? Pat!'

To make the game harder

Ask the children to rehearse in their head whether the word rhymes with their name.

Twenty questions

This fun, interactive game is a great way to develop children's questioning skills while improving their knowledge of rhyming words.

⭐ Resources

None

⭐ How to play

Divide the group into two teams. Think of a noun that the children are familiar with. Tell the group a word that rhymes with the noun. Each team takes a turn to ask up to twenty questions to try to find out what your word is. You can answer only yes or no to the questions. For instance, if your noun is **fish**, your rhyming clue could be **wish**. The group could then start asking questions such as 'Is it in this room?', 'Is it an animal?', 'Can you eat it?' The first team to work out your word is awarded a point. Continue playing as long as you like, depending on time available.

To make the game easier

To help the group, display some pictures of the nouns you may choose as your target word.

To make the game harder

The team that correctly guesses your word has to think of the next word for the remaining team to guess. They must provide the opposing team with a rhyming clue and correct answers to their questions.

Splat!

This game helps to improve the children's ability to listen for and detect rhyming words.

⭐ Resources

Selection of pictures; sticky tape; word lists (see next page). The pictures can be from magazines, the Internet or clip art software.

⭐ How to play

Fix one to four pictures on a wall with sticky tape. Divide the group into two teams and tell them to form a line. Number those in each team, starting at 1. Ask the no. 1s from each team to step forward to the pictures on the wall. Say a word that rhymes with one of the pictures on the wall. The word you say can be a nonsense word. The first child to say 'Splat' and put their hand on the picture that rhymes with the word you said wins a point for their team. You can decide whether or not to allow the rest of the team to help their member with the answer. The no. 1s then return to the end of the line and the no. 2s step up for the next rhyming word. Continue until all the team members have had a turn. You may decide to change the pictures on the wall as the game carries on.

To make the game easier

Reduce the number of picture choices for each team. For instance, you may decide to play the game using only two pictures. As the children's rhyming knowledge improves, you can gradually increase the number of pictures on the wall.

To make the game harder

The team members who have been called up to the wall are not allowed to get advice from the rest of their team.

Easier word list

✪ cat   ✪ hen   ✪ house   ✪ bee
✪ bear   ✪ mug   ✪ egg   ✪ eye
✪ fish   ✪ four   ✪ sun

Harder word list

✪ table   ✪ cooker   ✪ paper   ✪ kettle
✪ seven   ✪ donkey   ✪ scissors   ✪ cracker
✪ garden   ✪ coffee   ✪ party   ✪ jumper

Face down

This game is a great way to build the children's memory and rhyming skills.

⭐ Resources

Pairs of rhyming pictures (see page 141)

⭐ How to play

This game is best suited for up to five children. Put all the pictures face down on the table or floor. Ask a child to turn over two of the picture cards. If the pictures rhyme, that child can keep the cards. If the cards do not rhyme, they are turned face down and returned to their original spaces. The game continues until all the cards have been matched up with their rhyming pair.

Encourage the children to name the pictures as they turn them over and determine whether or not they rhyme. The rest of the group should be paying special attention to where the various cards are placed. Encourage the children to say the words and to listen to each other to check if the words rhyme.

To make the game easier

Before starting the game, name all of the picture cards with the group. You may also find it helpful to draw their attention to those pictures that rhyme with one another. Then shuffle the cards and play the game as explained above.

To make the game harder

Once the child has found a pair, ask them to think of one other word which also rhymes with the pictures they've picked up.

Rhymes in circles

This rhyming game is a great way for children to learn from their peers.

⭐ Resources

None

⭐ How to play

Ask the children to sit in a circle and choose one child to be in the middle. Tell the child in the middle to point to another child whilst you say a simple word; consonant–vowel–consonant words are ideal for this game. The child who is pointed at must then call out a word that rhymes with the word given. If that child cannot think of a rhyming word, or says a word that does not rhyme, another child is chosen. When the child who is pointed at can generate a rhyming word, they have a turn in the middle. The game continues until everyone has had a turn sitting in the middle of the circle.

To make the game easier

Tell the children that they can say rhyming words that are nonsense words. Encourage the group to try saying the rhyming pairs together so they can hear whether the two words sound alike. You may want to encourage the other children in the circle to help a child who is struggling.

To make the game harder

Ask the child who is pointed at to say two rhyming words instead of one.

Rhyming consequences

In this game the children work with a partner to generate rhymes for a target word.

⭐ Resources

Flipchart; pencils and paper

⭐ How to play

Write a consonant–vowel–consonant word such as **hen** on a flipchart. Put the children in pairs. Give each child a pencil and a piece of paper and ask them to write down the word from the flipchart. They must then fold their paper over to cover the word and write a word that rhymes with **hen** underneath the fold. This word is then folded over so that it cannot be seen and the paper is passed to their partner. The partner writes another word that rhymes with **hen** without knowing what their partner has written. In this instance, it may or may not be the same word. The paper is then returned to the original child, who writes another rhyming word for **hen**. The passing of the paper and the writing down of the rhyming words continues until the paper has been folded many times and there are lots of words on it that rhyme with **hen**. When the paper is full, ask the children to open it and read all of the rhyming words.

To make the game easier

Write the word on the flipchart. As a group, generate a list of rhyming words for the target word. Then play the game as explained above. The children will find it easier to generate some rhyming words because they have just heard them.

To make the game harder

To make the game more challenging, tell the children to write down the words within a time limit.

Make it up!

Children will enjoy making words together in this game.

⭐ Resources

Letter cards (see page 136); pencils and paper

⭐ How to play

Divide the children into teams of four. Depending on the size of your group, you may choose to make the teams larger or smaller. Give each team three different consonant cards and one vowel card. Explain that each team will work together to make as many different words as they can with their four letters. Appoint a scribe for each team to write their words down.

Encourage the children to discuss their words in their team and to say the words out loud. After a few minutes, ask a volunteer from each team to read their word list to the other groups and see who has the most words. Before each game begins, you should clarify whether or not nonsense words will be accepted. Keep in mind that making nonsense words creates valuable opportunities for the team to blend phonemes, which is an important skill. If you exclude nonsense words, you may need to select the cards you give each group.

To make the game easier

Play the game as a whole-group activity. Write the four letters on a whiteboard and ask the children to combine the sounds to form words. Record these words on the whiteboard. This is a great opportunity to begin a discussion about English words and nonsense words.

To make the game harder

To make the game really challenging, ask the group to blend the sounds without saying them. After a short interval, they can share the word they created with their scribe, who writes a list of them.

Hide and seek

This game helps children practise syllable deletion with the aid of picture cues.

⭐ Resources

Pictures relating to compound words such as:

- bookworm
- cowboy
- earring
- earthquake
- firefly
- football
- lighthouse
- peanut
- postman
- rainbow
- starfish
- suitcase
- sunlight
- teacup
- toothbrush
- warthog.

See page 142 for a small selection of pictures to help you get started with this game.

⭐ How to play

Before the children arrive, arrange the pictures in various places around the room so that they are partially hidden. When the children come in, choose one child to find a picture. When a picture has been found, they should hold it up for the rest of the group to see. The child who found the picture should then name it. Then ask them to repeat the word, omitting part of it; for example:

- Say **blackbird** without saying **black**.
- Say **handbag** without saying **bag**.
- Say **sandpit** without saying **sand**.

Encourage the rest of the group to listen carefully and think of their answer. After the child has answered, the other children can show their agreement by giving a thumbs up. If they don't agree they keep their hands in their lap. The game continues until all the pictures have been found.

To make the game easier

When a picture has been found and named, everyone in the group is encouraged to say and clap the number of syllables in the word. This helps to reinforce the concept of the word being segmented. Then everyone identifies and says the syllables in the word. For example, **black-bird, hand-bag, sand-pit**.

Now ask the child who found the picture or the small group to try to say the word as required in the main game, so that they can practise deleting syllables.

To make the game harder

Ask the child who found the picture to decide on the reply without saying the whole word, so that they have to rely on their knowledge of the word structure.

More words

- ✪ basketball
- ✪ blackberry
- ✪ butterfly
- ✪ dishwasher

- ✪ fingerprint
- ✪ grasshopper
- ✪ handwriting
- ✪ newspaper

- ✪ rattlesnake
- ✪ sunflower
- ✪ waterfall
- ✪ zookeeper

Change up

This game teaches children how to blend phonemes.

⭐ Resources

Game cards (see page 143); pens and paper

⭐ How to play

Divide the children into teams of four and give each team six game cards face down. You can adjust this, depending on the size of your group. Tell each team to sit in a circle. Explain that you will give them a word and that their task is to change the first or last sound in the word. Choose a scribe in each group to write the words down as they go. Choose one child from each team and tell them their word, for example, **hen**. That child turns a game card over and changes the word **hen** according to the instructions on it. For instance, if it says 'start the word with p', the child changes **hen** to **pen**. The next child in that team turns over another card. If the next card says 'end the word with sh' the child would change **pen** to **pesh**. Each team continues playing until all of the game cards have been used up.

Remind the children that some of the words they make will be nonsense words. Encourage the teams to try to say the words they are creating. When each group has finished, ask the scribe to read their word list to the other groups.

If there is time available, shuffle the cards and deal out a different set to each team. Appoint a different scribe. Ask them to create another chain of words with a new consonant–vowel–consonant word provided by you.

To make the game easier

Play the game as a whole group. Give the children a consonant–vowel–consonant word and ask them to take turns drawing a card. Who can work out what the word changes into? Encourage the children to say the answer for the whole group to hear. Write each of the words on a whiteboard, so they can see the changes.

To make the game harder

To make the game really challenging, ask the group to blend the sounds without saying the words. After a minute or two, the scribe asks each member of the group in turn to share their word change with the rest of the group. The scribe records each new word.

Musical pairs

Children will enjoy working with partners to form words with different phonemes.

⭐ Resources

Phoneme cards (see page 136); music CD or cassette; CD or cassette player

⭐ How to play

Give each child a phoneme card. To ensure that they can properly identify the phoneme, ask them to say the sound. Tell the children that they're going to play a game. When the music starts, they can dance around the room. When the music stops, they pair up with the child closest to them. If there is an odd number of children in the group, you will need to pair up with one of the children. The two children look at each other's phonemes and work out whether they could combine their sounds to form a word. For instance, if **sh** and **f** pair up, they could say **fish**, or **chef**.

You can draw attention to spelling anomalies if you wish, but keep in mind that the purpose of this game is to blend phonemes. If the pair can think of a word which has their phonemes in it, they say their word. If the pair is not able to think of a word, they are out of the game and sit down. The game continues until there is only one pair of children left.

Encourage the children to try saying different words and sounds. You may decide to accept nonsense words from the pairs, as this demonstrates good blending skills.

To make the game easier

If when the music stops a pair of children cannot form a word, you can give them a choice of two words. The first word would use both of the phonemes and be a correct answer. The second word would use only one of the phonemes and would be an incorrect answer. For instance, if the pair has the phonemes **g** and **m**, you could ask them 'Which one of these has both of your sounds, **game** or **gut**?' The pair must decide which word is correct. If they choose the correct answer, they can continue playing the game.

To make the game harder

Ask the pair to think of two words that combine each of the phonemes. For instance, if the phonemes are **t** and **l**, the pair might come up with the words **let** and **tail**.

Fun with names

In this game, the children will practise phoneme manipulation with their names. Be sensitive to individual names to avoid distress.

⭐ Resources

None

⭐ How to play

The aim of the game is for the group to practise phoneme deletion and manipulation. Tell the children that you going to play a name game. They must change the first or last sound of their first name. Give the group a target sound, such as **p**. In this instance, the children must delete the first sound in their name and replace it with **p**. Therefore, Beth becomes Peth, Dale becomes Pale, and so on. Point to each child and encourage them to say their altered name so that the rest of the group can hear it.

Suggested variations

✪ Delete the first sound in the child's first name: Sam become Am, Leena becomes Eena, and so on.
✪ Delete the first sound in the name and start it with **b**, **f**, **m** or **p**.
✪ Delete the last sound in the name and end it with **sh**, **m** or **t**.
✪ If the child has a multisyllabic name, ask them to shorten it by saying just the first syllable of their name.

To make the game easier

Ask the children to change only the initial sound of their name.

To make the game harder

Ask the children to work out their changed name in their head. As an additional challenge, ask them to change their surname, too. Choose some children to share what they have thought of.

I'm going to the moon

This game will help improve the children's memory while providing them with an opportunity to manipulate phonemes.

⭐ Resources

None

⭐ How to play

Start the game off by saying 'I'm going to the moon and I'm taking a pin.' The next child has to repeat what you said and add another word. When the child adds their word, however, they must change one of the phonemes of your word. For instance, they might say 'I'm going to the moon and I'm taking a pin and a tin.' The next child might say 'I'm going to the moon and I'm taking a pin and a tin and a tick.' Depending on the size of your group and the time available, continue until all of the children have had a turn. Encourage the children to say all the words while playing the game, and to think about the phoneme that has been changed.

To make the game easier

Write all of the words on a flipchart as the children change the phonemes. This will give the group visual support for the task. Talk with the children about taking one sound away and substituting different sounds until they're able to get a real word.

To make the game harder

Ask the children to work out how they're going to change the word in their head when they have their turn, as this makes them rely on their phonic knowledge.

Fill in the sound

Children will enjoy working together in this game to form words with different phonemes.

⭐ Resources

None

⭐ How to play

Choose three children to stand in front of the group. Give each of the first two children a sound to remember, such as **p** and **a**. Encourage the group to choose a third letter or phoneme to make a word with the other two letters. Once the group has decided upon a third letter or phoneme, the third child represents the third sound. The children then arrange themselves in the correct order, so that they can say their sounds to form a word such as **pat**, **pan** or **pack**. The act of moving, saying individual sounds and then blending the sounds together in the right order helps children with the concept of blending phonemes. Keep in mind that the three children can stand in any order, as long as that correlates with one of the words suggested. For instance, if they have **p**, **t** and **a** they could rearrange themselves to spell **pat**, **tap** or **apt**.

To make the game easier

In this version give each of the two children a consonant to use, and ask the rest of the group to create as many words as possible by inserting a vowel of their choice between combinations of these two letters.

To make the game harder

Choose four children to stand in front of the group. Give three of the children a phoneme each. Ask the group to generate as many different word combinations as they can by adding one other phoneme to their group. For instance, give the group **s**, **t** and **e**. The group chooses to add **m** or **p** to make **stem** or **step**. An additional challenge is to ask the children to play the game as above but ask them to add a consonant blend at the beginning of the word to make consonant–consonant–vowel–consonant words.

Spot the difference

This game will improve the children's listening skills and help them to discriminate between phonemes better.

⭐ Resources

Flipchart; pen

⭐ How to play

This game works best as a whole-group activity. Tell the children that you are going to say two words. They are to work out the difference between the two words. For instance, if you said **sand** and **band** they must recognise that the first sound was changed; it was **s** and is now **b**. It may be necessary to ask some questions to prompt a response from the group. For example:

✪ Where did the sound change?
✪ Was the sound that changed at the beginning or the end of the word?
✪ Did the vowel sound change?
✪ What sounds were swapped?

Once the children have listened to the words a couple of times, you may want to write the two words on a flipchart. This will help them grasp the concept of phonemes and graphemes changing. Take care not to change the game into a spelling activity; its primary focus is to have the children listen for differences in the word.

This is a useful activity to target a particular group of sounds that need working on.

To make the game easier

Restrict the word pairs to words that are spelt without phonetic irregularities. This will enable you to write them on the flipchart and demonstrate that when the letters are changed, the sounds change too.

To make the game harder

Challenge the group to work out how the word has changed as a silent task. Then ask them to share their responses with the rest of the children.

Suggested word lists

❂ p/b initial discrimination: pit/bit, pad/bad, pin/bin, pie/buy
❂ t/d word final discrimination: sat/sad, bat/bad, mat/mad, hat/had
❂ vowel discrimination: pen/pin, ten/tan, fun/fan, hot/hat
❂ general word initial discrimination: fat/cat, shy/my, dig/wig, hen/men, door/four, thin/bin
❂ final discrimination: cart/card, cake/came, dish/dip, ball/bought, laugh/lap, bird/burn, bus/but.

Same or different

This game is an easy way to help children listen for the similarities and differences in words.

⭐ Resources

None

⭐ How to play

This is a quick game to help fill a few minutes. Start the game by saying a pair of words which either sound the same or are subtly different. For example, the words that are different could have just one phoneme that's different between them, such as **pat** and **mat**. Ask the children to listen carefully to your words and call out 'same' if they sound the same or 'different' if they sound different. You can make the task harder or easier depending on the type of phonemes that are different in each word. For instance, vowel sounds are harder to discriminate between than initial consonant sounds.

To make the game easier

Start the game by saying just individual phonemes. The children's task is to determine whether they are the same or different. Some pairs to start with are **p–p**, **t–m**, **b–d** and **sh–sh**. Once the group can discriminate between phonemes, start introducing consonant–vowel combinations such as **dee–hee**, **my–my**, **bor–por** and **go–do**. You can gradually increase the difficulty of the game by using consonant–vowel–consonant words such as **ham–him**, **sap–sat**, and so on. You may want to include a step for focusing on the final consonant by discriminating between vowel–consonant combinations such as **ate** and **ape** and **am** and **at**.

To make the game harder

In addition to asking them if the word is the same or different, ask the children to tell you what sound has changed.

Standing phonemes

Children will enjoy learning how to segment and blend phonemes in this game.

⭐ Resources

None

⭐ How to play

Ask three children to form a line and count 'One, two, three,' then break a consonant–vowel–consonant word down into its sounds. For instance, for **fit**, child 1 would say **f**, child 2 **i** and child 3 **t**. Ask the rest to try to do the same. When they understand this, put them into teams of three. Give each a different consonant–vowel–consonant word to break down and practise saying. Each group can then perform their word.

Suggested word list

✪ bed	✪ cup	✪ lit	✪ pin
✪ bug	✪ fig	✪ mop	✪ sun
✪ bus	✪ fin	✪ mouth	✪ tap
✪ cake	✪ hall	✪ pen	

To make the game easier

Do the activity as a whole group, using three different children each time.

To make the game harder

Use two-syllable words or words with consonant blends or clusters. You may need to assign six to eight children to each group.

Suggested word list

✪ b-l-a-ck	✪ d-e-n-t-i-s-t	✪ s-t-a-m-p
✪ b-u-n-k-b-e-d	✪ f-r-a-me	✪ s-t-e-p
✪ ch-a-tt-er	✪ sh-e-l-f	✪ th-r-ee

What's changed?

This game is a simple and constructive way to teach the children how to segment phonemes.

✪ Resources

Word cards (see page 144); pencils and paper

✪ How to play

Put the children in pairs. Give each child a word card from a pair. The words must sound similar but have one phoneme between them that's different. See the word list below for pairs. Ask the children to draw a picture to represent their words. Then tell them to swap their picture with their partner. Each must now work out which phoneme in the word has changed. Repeat with different pairs of words until the group has seen all the pictures.

Word cards

- ✪ cap and map
- ✪ harp and heart
- ✪ moon and man
- ✪ bun and bug

- ✪ red and head
- ✪ dot and doll
- ✪ pip and pop
- ✪ poor and four

- ✪ lolly and holly
- ✪ game and gate
- ✪ seat and beat
- ✪ sock and sick

To make the game easier

Give each pair of children word cards that rhyme. This requires them to decide only how the initial sound has changed. For instance:

- ✪ bed and head
- ✪ fat and mat

- ✪ dog and log
- ✪ back and pack

- ✪ fan and pan.

To make the game harder

After swapping their drawings, ask the children to think of and draw two other words which are similar but have one phoneme that's different between them, such as **mat** and **map**.

Word transformation

This game is an interactive way to teach children about the patterns in words.

⭐ Resources

Pencils and paper

⭐ How to play

Put the children in pairs. Give each pair a consonant–vowel–consonant word and a pencil and paper. Ask them to change their word, one letter at a time, a total of three times. For instance, if the pair starts with the word **dog**, their sequence might look something like this: **fog**, **fig**, **fin**. Or if they start with the word **cat**, their sequence might look like this: **hat**, **hit**, **hip**. The children should record the sequence of changes on their paper. After each pair has changed their word and recorded the changes, ask a couple of the pairs to share their word transformations with the rest of the group.

To make the game easier

Instead of asking the children to work in pairs, do this activity as a whole group. Record the changes on a flipchart for everyone to see.

To make the game harder

After each pair has changed their word and recorded the changes, ask them to write their first and last words on a separate piece of paper. The pair must then swap this paper with another pair. Each pair's task is now to try to work out the other pair's middle two words. For instance, if one pair receives a piece of paper with the words **dog** and **pin**, they should try to decide how the word **dog** and the subsequent words were changed to get to the word **pin**.

Template for making a die

Permission to Photocopy

Number lines

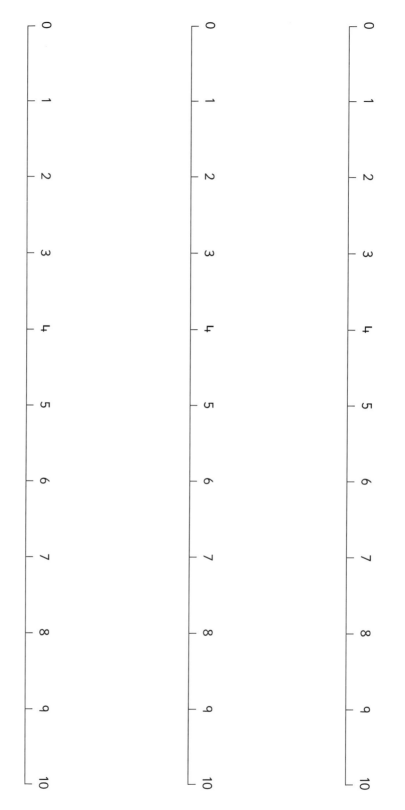

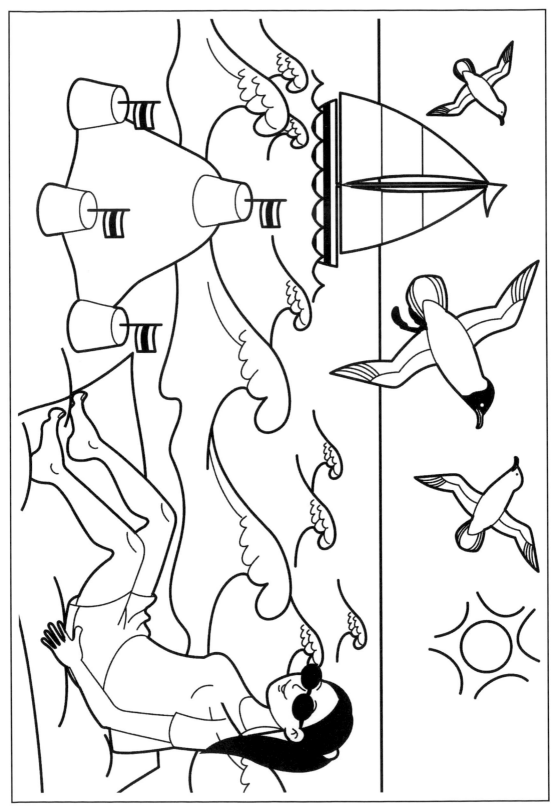

Permission to Photocopy

Fruits	Vegetables	Boys' names
Girls' names	Countries	Places to visit
Items of clothing	Things at school	Animals
Things you can hear	Things that are red	Names of drinks
Sports	Things in a house	Things at the zoo
Television programmes	Films	Things with wheels

a	b	c
d	e	f
g	h	i
j	k	l
m	n	o
p	q	r
s	t	u
v	w	x
y	z	ch
sh	th	wh

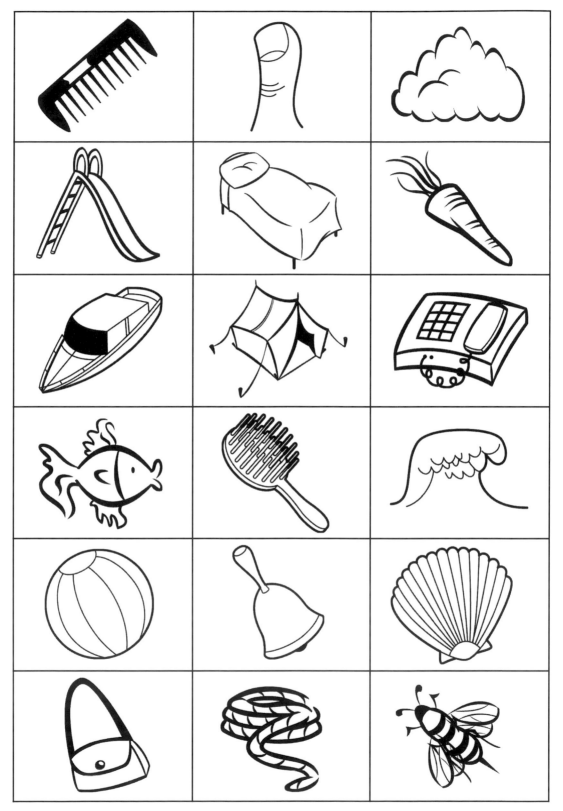

Pairs of pictures with the same final sound

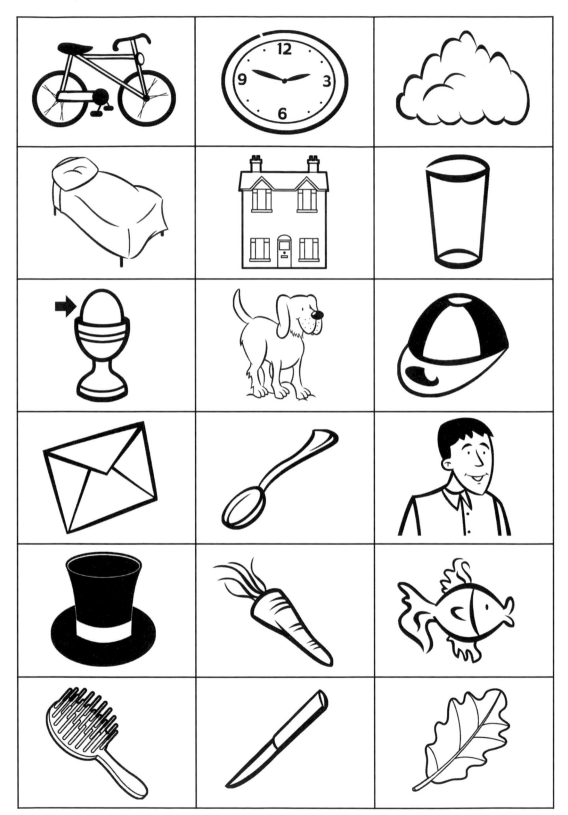

Permission to Photocopy

Permission to Photocopy

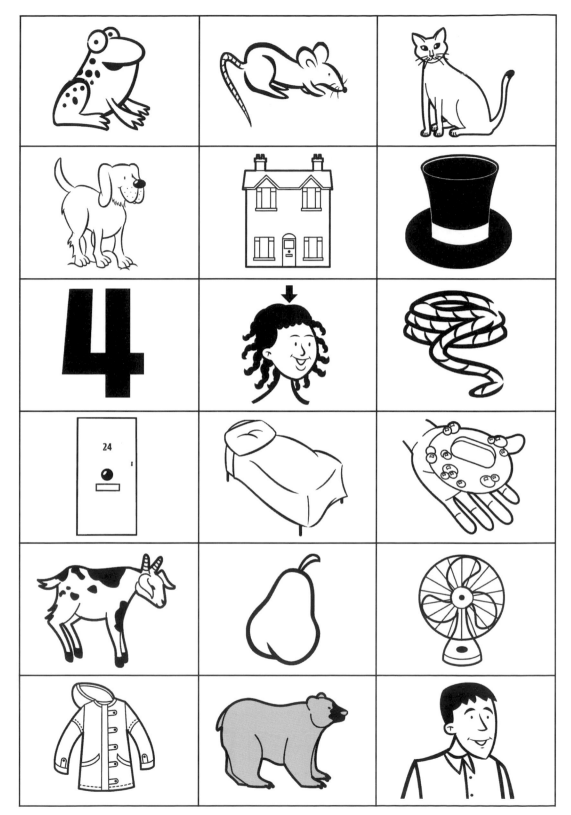

Start the word with **d**	Start the word with **p**	Start the word with **t**	Start the word with **m**
Start the word with **s**	Start the word with **f**	Start the word with **g**	Start the word with **l**
Start the word with **b**	End the word with **t**	End the word with **p**	End the word with **n**
End the word with **sh**	End the word with **d**	End the word with **ck**	End the word with **g**

cap	harp	moon
map	heart	man
bun	red	dot
bug	head	doll
pip	poor	lolly
pop	four	holly
game	seat	sock
gate	beat	sick